Praise for

"This series provides a practical and _____ _____ _____ reading _____
today." – John V. Biernacki, Partner, Jones Day

"*Inside the Minds* draws from the collective experience of the best professionals. The books are informative from an academic, and, more importantly, practical perspective. I highly recommend them." – Keith M. Aurzada, Partner, Bryan Cave LLP

"Aspatore's *Inside the Minds* series provides practical, cutting edge advice from those with insight into the real world challenges that confront businesses in the global economy." – Michael Bednarek, Partner, Shearman & Sterling LLP

"What to read when you want to be in the know—topical, current, practical, and useful information on areas of the law that everyone is talking about." – Erika L. Morabito, Partner, Patton Boggs LLP

"Some of the best insight around from sources in the know" – Donald R. Kirk, Shareholder, Fowler White Boggs PA

"The *Inside the Minds* series provides a unique window into the strategic thinking of key players in business and law." – John M. Sylvester, Partner, K&L Gates LLP

"Comprehensive analysis and strategies you won't find anywhere else." – Stephen C. Stapleton, Of Counsel, Dykema Gossett PLLC

"The *Inside the Minds* series is a real hands-on, practical resource for cutting edge issues." – Trey Monsour, Partner, Haynes and Boone LLP

"A tremendous resource, amalgamating commentary from leading professionals that is presented in a concise, easy to read format." – Alan H. Aronson, Shareholder, Akerman Senterfitt

"Unique and invaluable opportunity to gain insight into the minds of experienced professionals." – Jura C. Zibas, Partner, Lewis Brisbois Bisgaard & Smith LLP

"A refreshing collection of strategic insights, not dreary commonplaces, from some of the best of the profession." – Roger J. Magnuson, Partner, Dorsey & Whitney LLP

"Provides valuable insights by experienced practitioners into practical and theoretical developments in today's ever-changing legal world." – Elizabeth Gray, Partner, Willkie, Farr & Gallagher LLP

"This series provides invaluable insight into the practical experiences of lawyers in the trenches." – Thomas H. Christopher, Partner, Kilpatrick Stockton LLP

ASPATORE

Aspatore Books, a Thomson Reuters business, exclusively publishes C-Level executives and partners from the world's most respected companies and law firms. Each publication provides professionals of all levels with proven business and legal intelligence from industry insiders—direct and unfiltered insight from those who know it best. Aspatore Books is committed to publishing an innovative line of business and legal titles that lay forth principles and offer insights that can have a direct financial impact on the reader's business objectives.

Each chapter in the *Inside the Minds* series offers thought leadership and expert analysis on an industry, profession, or topic, providing a future-oriented perspective and proven strategies for success. Each author has been selected based on their experience and C-Level standing within the business and legal communities. *Inside the Minds* was conceived to give a first-hand look into the leading minds of top business executives and lawyers worldwide, presenting an unprecedented collection of views on various industries and professions.

INSIDE THE MINDS

Best Practices for Managing Outsourcing Transactions

Leading Lawyers on Selecting Appropriate Providers and Creating Flexible Service-Level Agreements

ASPATORE

For additional copies or customer service inquiries, please e-mail west.customer.service@thomson.com.

ISBN 978-0-314-29227-8

Mat #41662347

Contents

A Practical Guide to Risk Management in Global Outsourcing

Harry Rubin

Partner

Ropes & Gray LLP

ASPATORE

Introduction

In recent years, I have worked on numerous cross-border outsourcings for the development of customized software products and technology systems, manufacturing arrangements, and a wide spectrum of diverse business services, ranging from accounting and back office functions to comprehensive business services for the manufacturing, financial, and travel industries. There is a consistent and gradual increase in application software development, business process, and manufacturing outsourcing for small- and medium-sized companies. Outsourcing has become truly global, extending far beyond India and China, with Central and Eastern Europe, Latin America, and other Asian countries increasingly playing key roles.

Economic factors continue to play a central role in outsourcing, including cost differentials in manufacturing and labor. Many countries have public policies fostering technology development and information technology (IT) services. Indeed, as China and India have matured, countries in Eastern Europe and Latin America have followed suit and now offer equal or better cost savings and structural efficiencies. It is increasingly common to find key vendors in India sub-sourcing their services to other newly emerging outsourcing vendor countries, such as Vietnam.

With this in mind, outsourcing clients must focus on potential legal complexities and corresponding risk mitigation strategies. Although English is used to negotiate and draft agreements, and both vendors and customers use Anglo-American agreements, material jurisdictional differences remain in key legal areas, including intellectual property (IP), competition and employment law and applicable business practices. As many salient aspects of an outsourcing transaction are sensitive to the impact of the vendor country's laws, a customer cannot simply expect to use globally US-based agreements. Clients must retain experienced counsel to apprise them of the risks they will face in certain jurisdictions under local laws.

Helping a Client Decide Whether to Outsource

Deciding when and what to outsource is a critical threshold question. Companies used to consider outsourcing exclusively as a cost-savings device, but this is no longer the case. Even if outsourcing is undertaken solely for cost savings, the impact of the outsourcing is potentially dramatically more far-reaching, sometimes amounting more to a *de facto* corporate restructuring than a service arrangement. Outsourcing may have long-term consequences for the customer's structure operations, human relations, service offerings, and products.

The ability to predict future outsourcing needs often depends heavily on the company's strategic vision. In addition to the ability to capitalize on cost differentials, outsourcing is more likely to make sense if the company is growing extensively such that it no longer has the bandwidth to perform certain operations well; if it is expanding into non-core areas requiring the expertise of an outsourcing vendor; or if it seeks to refocus only on its core competencies and wishes to divest itself of non-core, but business material, functions. Outsourcing may also be beneficial for a company moving to a new geographic location, where it is best to have the work done onsite. At the extreme, however, there is the danger of "over-sourcing." If a company outsources nearly everything it does, the company may be better served by restructuring or selling itself. Significantly, the question "what's left?" is as important as what will be outsourced.

Companies with the most success in outsourcing are those that did not need to search for reasons to outsource. It has been perfectly obvious to them that there are certain things others can do better—with superior expertise, IP, employees, or pricing. Those companies did not outsource their core functions, but instead are focused on their core business by finding someone else to handle important ancillary operations.

Customers often fail to consider the complexities of transitioning their existing operations to an outsourcing vendor. Due to the potentially transformative impact of an outsourcing, clients must assess the effect an outsourcing may have on their organization and how it will be perceived *internally* and *externally*. Will the company be perceived as fundamentally changing its services, products, or entire business orientation or will the outsourcing be perceived as a means to improve efficiency? The external perception of the outsourcing may have far-reaching implications for the client's customers, suppliers, and other relationships. The company should be prepared to address these issues internally and externally with coherent and proactive messaging.

Conducting Due Diligence to Select an Appropriate Provider

Potential outsourcing vendors must be carefully vetted with particular focus on their reputations and performance and litigation records. A simple Google search may yield a wealth of information. Areas for diligence should include the potential vendor's record with customers, reference checks, the vendor's core competencies, levels of expertise and experience, how the vendor is structured, and identification of the key vendor employees the client should seek out. Particularly crucial is ascertaining whether the vendor has the financial strength to stand behind its contractual obligations. Depending on the size of the transaction, it is important to conduct extensive interviews with each potential vendor and implement a formal request for proposals (RFP) competitive bidding process. The RFP should be vigorously managed and streamlined to allow for the methodical comparative evaluation of each vendor across all salient business, technical, financial, and legal parameters.

Utilizing an Outsourcing Team

The customer should assemble a team including technical, financial, and business managers as well as in-house and outside legal counsel. It is also essential to engage outside technology consultants to address the operational and technological questions related to the outsourcing. A systems integrator is frequently imperative in bringing together the various aspects of the outsourcing and ensuring that everything works in harmony with the client's existing systems. The client team should form a comprehensive consensus regarding the business, financial, and legal terms of the outsourcing. The client's chief operating officer, chief technology officer, and other senior executives should ultimately participate in the outsourcing provider selection, including, as appropriate, interviewing and assessing vendors, developing the technical aspects of the RFP, and working closely with counsel.

The legal terms and technical and financial aspects of the outsourcing must reinforce and complement one another. This requires the legal team to understand what the technical issues are, and the technical team to understand the representations, warranties, indemnities, and IP aspects of the relationship. The financial considerations are overriding, and everybody working on the outsourcing deal should communicate frequently to ensure complete coordination.

Managing the Risks and Challenges Related to Outsourcing

With its opportunities, outsourcing poses considerable challenges and risks. These may best be analyzed through a five-dimensional risk prism, evaluating (i) performance, (ii) IP, (iii) liability, (iv) enforcement, and (v) business continuity.

Managing Performance Risk

Will the vendor actually perform? To address this risk, the service level agreement (SLA) attached to the outsourcing contract must set forth the technical specifications, acceptance criteria, other pertinent requirements and pricing terms. As applicable, the SLA should cover specifications for prototypes and finished products, data, services, software, and IT systems. The SLA must be detailed and well thought out, written in concise contractual language with clear obligations to perform, and contain the appropriate incentives. The SLA should be drafted as a legally binding and coherent long-term implementation plan for the outsourcing.

Payment provisions must be comprehensively and strategically considered, including with respect to vendor bonuses, re-performance credits, and benchmarking provisions.

The agreement's warranty section should cover the following categories: (i) authorization, including the power and proper organization of the parties and ability to enter into and perform, (ii) compliance with applicable laws and regulations, including in particular privacy and data security and critical standard operating procedures, (iii) IP non-infringement; and (iv) performance of services and deliverables. The remedies section should clarify the vendor's obligations with respect to re-performance, repair, replacement, and what remedies the customer should have by way of termination or refund in the event of breaches and epidemic product or service failures.

Of critical importance in managing performance risk is the change order mechanism. Both parties should be able to enter into mutually agreed change orders. Moreover, a client should insist on the ability to require a vendor to comply with mandatory change orders requested by the client because of material changes in applicable laws or critical unforeseen business exigencies. These can be quite controversial and, as a result, the vendor would expect, and the customer should agree, to pay appropriate compensation for the implementation of mandatory change orders.

Managing Intellectual Property Risk

The second risk dimension is IP risk, which should be viewed as a "three-legged stool" covering IP, confidentiality, and non-competition. They each work in tandem and supplement one another. Both parties should avoid joint ownership of IP, if IP is created in the course of the parties' collaboration in the outsourcing. Instead, one party should own the IP and the other party should obtain broad perpetual, worldwide, and fully paid cross licenses.

The confidentiality section is exceptionally important due to the potential application of the vendor's home laws. The agreement should not contain a standard US-based boilerplate provision. The confidentiality provision should specify in robust detail the scope of confidential information—including trade secrets, know how, third-party data, and IP—that is provided by one party to the other or created by both parties. Computer access should be controlled. Services should be performed at dedicated sites and suitable security protection should be implemented and required by the agreement.

It will be difficult for a client to impose rigorous non-compete provisions on major or established vendors. Sometimes, however, it will be possible at least to ensure that key employees working on the customer's project will not work on competitive accounts.

Significantly, the client must confirm that the IP assignment, confidentiality, and non-compete provisions are enforceable in accordance with its terms. This requires a thorough understanding of the applicable laws of the vendor's jurisdiction. The inclusion of "magic words" may be required. Vendor employees may need to sign individual agreements. Particular attention must be paid to the laws of India, China, and several Latin

American countries in that context. In general, the non-compete provision must be reasonable under the circumstances in terms of scope, duration, and geographic reach.

Managing Liability Risk

Liability is the third risk perspective, with another three-legged stool rearing its head: indemnity, liability, and liability caps/exclusions. The parties must negotiate how they will allocate responsibilities and liabilities in a range of areas, from violations of applicable law and third-party rights, to breaches of the agreement and performance obligations. Highly contentious, due to their potentially severe financial implications, are caps on liabilities and exceptions to those caps, and who bears what risk under what circumstances. In general, one would expect liabilities and indemnities to cover key enumerated provisions such as third-party IP breaches, breaches of privacy and security and applicable laws, and claims by employees and subcontractors. While the vendor will insist on comprehensive liability caps and certainly would want to ensure that its liability does not exceed the contract value, the customer should try to ensure that at least material breaches such as violations of applicable law privacy and security breaches and third-party IP infringements would not be capped.

Managing Enforcement Risk

The fourth area of risk management centers on the very ability to enforce the agreement. It requires not just an understanding of the law governing the agreement, but the extent to which it is possible to control its applicable legal environment. An especially important consideration is whether the client will be working with a vendor based overseas, but contracting with a holding or shell company in the United States. If so, the overseas vendor (the parent company) should be required to sign the agreement to ensure the contracting party is the party against which the client can practically and legally enforce the agreement.

The procedures for managing the outsourcing and resolving disputes should be thought through in detail, particularly because the outsourcing ultimately is an iterative process and the agreement will not be able to predict all contentious issues, let alone resolve their outcome. As such, a procedure for managing the relationship and resolving disputes effectively and efficiently before formal legal proceedings is essential. Preliminarily, the parties should each have a technical management team that deals with such matters. The matters then should be delegated to senior executives. Ultimately, arbitration or litigation should ensue.

Managing Business-Continuing Risk

Finally, the fifth and frequently most overlooked or understated dimension of risk is business-continuing risk. Of concern is if the client may terminate or extend the relationship, and how a client can ensure its ability to continue operating seamlessly, on a turnkey basis, prior to and after termination. The agreement must ensure the continuity of operations during the transition to and from outsourcing. One way to achieve this is to provide for the ability of the client unilaterally to extend the term of the agreement—even if the cost is high and, as a minimum, there should be a comfortably long post-termination transition period. The agreement should list the vendor employees who will work on the project during the transition and state the vendor's obligation to cooperate with the client in transitioning the outsourcing to either the client or the client's designee in a manner that ensures continuity. Additionally, it is important to consider which IP technology transfers and licenses the client may need and to clearly define the transition period. The client may even require facilities on a permanent or temporary basis.

Conclusion

Moving forward, small- and mid-level companies will outsource more of their functions. In addition, there is likely to be a proliferation of involvement by new players in Asia, Eastern Europe, and Latin America.

Key Takeaways

- When negotiating an outsourcing, remember that many key terms of the outsourcing transaction are sensitive to the impact of the vendor country's laws—do not simply expect that everything in a US-based agreement applies globally even if the agreement is governed by US law.

- Recommend outsourcing for a company that is growing rapidly, focusing on its core operation, expanding into areas where it is not an expert, or moving to a new geographic location. Think about what not to outsource and what will be left. If the client thinks it might want to outsource nearly everything the company does, the client might be better served by restructuring or selling.

- Encourage your client to have a team comprised of technology, financial, and business officers, outside technology consultants, and in-house and outside legal counsel *before* engaging in an outsourcing relationship. Such a team should generate a comprehensive strategic view regarding what is important, what is less important, and what is negotiable when approaching the arrangement.

- Clearly and comprehensively draft the outsourcing agreement to address five dimensions of risk: performance, intellectual property, liability, enforcement, and business continuity.

Harry Rubin is a partner and the co-chair of Ropes & Gray LLP's International Practice Group residing in the firm's New York office. He is a globally recognized authority on global technology transactions and former co-chair of the Technology Committee of the International Bar Association. Mr. Rubin has extensive experience in the representation of leading private equity and venture firms, technology and life sciences companies and technology users in acquisitions, mergers, spin-outs, strategic alliances, technology transfers, licensing, VAR, OEM, systems integration, applications development and maintenance and business process outsourcing, supply side manufacturing outsourcing, and IP protection and commercialization strategies. He is a frequent speaker and author on these topics. Mr. Rubin's book, International Technology Transfers, *is widely considered the standard reference text in the field.*

Mr. Rubin has received numerous leading professional honors and recognitions, including: Euromoney's Best of the Best USA, Elite Practitioner in Information Technology; The Best Lawyers in America, Information Technology Law; Intellectual Asset Management – A Guide to the World's 300 Leading IP Strategists ; Chambers USA: America's Leading Lawyers for Business; and New York and California Super Lawyers. *Mr. Rubin is a graduate of Harvard University and Columbia law School and is fluent in English, German, Hebrew, and French.*

Evolving Nature of Outsourcing Raises New Business and Legal Issues for Customers

Daniel R. Mummery

Partner

Gibson Dunn & Crutcher

ASPATORE

Introduction

Over the past few years, there has been a distinct shift in how customers approach outsourcing transactions. Historically, customers looked to outsourcing almost exclusively as a means to cut costs. This drive to reduce cost was often—although not always—completed at the expense of enhanced service delivery. Such deals often included some concept of improvement or transformation. While a customer hoped to obtain some transformational benefits from outsourcing to a qualified supplier, a failure to achieve these anticipated benefits was not likely to be fatal to the transaction, provided that the cost of the outsourced services reduced appropriately over the course of the customer/supplier relationship.

Today, more customers consider outsourcing as an integral part of a strategic plan. Customers are less focused on cost reduction and are instead placing greater emphasis on the overall value proposition, including the benefit of receiving additional or enhanced services. Even customers that prioritize cost reduction agree that savings alone is not a sufficient reason to outsource. Rather, customers are looking to suppliers to provide access to new technologies and specialized knowledge and expertise, increased flexibility and efficiency, and business transformation. Many customers are also looking for suppliers that can transform common services to standardized platforms, thus providing the customer with a range of additional potential benefits.

This change in approach, along with the continuing evolution of technology, has fundamentally reshaped how organizations contract for services. Many customers are moving away from big deals in which large parts of the organization are outsourced to a single supplier toward smaller, more strategic deals. The trend is to focus on areas where the customer believes that it will achieve the greatest benefit from enhanced or standardized services, including benefits at a financial, organizational, and service-delivery level. In line with this, customers are moving away from single-supplier arrangements to multi-supplier sourcing environments, building on a number of suppliers' different strengths to obtain better overall service quality. With this approach, customers are targeting those suppliers that have a higher degree of knowledge, expertise, and specialization in the area being outsourced. While there are many benefits to this model, multi-sourcing comes with significant costs and risks, particularly as customers need to allocate additional resources to manage, govern, integrate, and coordinate the different suppliers.

Along with this multi-sourcing approach, more customers are considering and implementing cloud-based solutions. Unlike traditional outsourcing, cloud-based offerings provide services (such as infrastructure, networks, and applications) under a utility model, allowing a customer to consume services and pay for them as they are consumed. While cloud or cloud services often refers to services made available through the Internet, the terms can also be used to describe all sorts of utility-based services where consumption and payment are aligned, and the capital cost is shifted to the supplier. Pay-per-use reflects one of the many benefits of cloud computing/utility computing, enabling customers to avoid the up-front investment of building on-premises infrastructure, integration costs, and ongoing information technology labor costs. Beyond the financial incentives, there are many other benefits of cloud computing/utility computing, including on-demand scalability/rapid elasticity, rapid access to updated versions, broad network access, resource pooling, and measured service. Of course, the use of such cloud services can lead to increasingly complex security, privacy, tax, and related compliance and control issues that need to be adequately addressed.

The decision about which functions to perform in-house and when to employ an external supplier is highly variable, depending on the customer's business. Many customers are still reluctant to outsource certain functions that they consider to be critical to the company's core business. As such, information technology and business process outsourcing transactions continue to be the most common. In the case of information technology outsourcing, a broad mix of services continues to be outsourced, although the trend is toward smaller and more focused deals rather than full-scope infrastructure and application development and maintenance deals. Business process outsourcing transactions cover a range of different business processes including traditional back office functions such as finance and accounting and procurement, as well as front office functions such as customer relations and marketing. As with information technology outsourcing, the trend with business process outsourcing is for customers to look to smaller, more targeted deals to focus on areas where they can get the most benefit from a sophisticated supplier—and this could be virtually any function, depending on the customer.

As customers have become increasingly comfortable with traditional areas of outsourcing, there has been a significant increase in knowledge process outsourcing. Knowledge process outsourcing has gained traction in the United States in recent years as customers look to outsource functions that demand more advanced research, technical, analytical, and decision-making skills. For example, in the financial services industry, outsourcing has expanded to common core middle office functions. Functions such as derivatives processing, collateral management, compliance monitoring, performance analytics, reconciliations, and client reporting are now being outsourced to third parties. While the buy-in of the middle office outsourcing model has been slow, largely due to the implicit nervousness about handing over responsibility of what is often perceived to be a core capability for an asset manager, there has been significant growth in middle office outsourcing both domestically and internationally. The key here, as with any sourcing transaction, is to weigh the advantages and disadvantages that could result from the specific transaction to determine whether the upside is worth the potential downside risk of the transaction. Even where such a review is favorable to the transaction, the business will have to ultimately decide whether it is willing to cede some level of day-to-day control, which inevitably comes with a sourcing transaction, to receive the anticipated benefits.

Noteworthy Issues and Trends

Balancing Scope, Performance, and Price

Scope, level of performance, and price reflect the key building blocks of each sourcing transaction regardless of whether the deal is a large-scale outsourcing, a multi-sourcing, the acquisition of cloud-based services, or some mix of all of these. The relationship between scope, level of performance, and price, and the final balance between them will be felt throughout the term. In this regard, the desired scope and level of performance will have a direct bearing on the final price offered by each supplier, with some variation to reflect solutioning, risk tolerance, and profit margin. While it may be possible to drive down price during negotiations, such reductions in price will eventually affect the ability of the supplier to deliver the desired services at the desired level of performance and prevent the parties from achieving a mutually beneficial relationship— that is, a deal in which the customer receives the services at a fair price and the supplier covers the cost of delivering those services and makes a reasonable margin on those services. Where the balance between scope, performance, and price is right, customers are more likely to receive the benefit of additional value-added services as well as additional services at no charge. Where the balance is wrong, both the services delivered and the performance of those services can suffer—at worst a never-ending cycle of change orders is the outcome, where every little addition beyond the existing scope necessitates an increase in the fees charged by the supplier. As a result, while customers still focus on the bottom line, it is less of a driver and is now one of the many factors considered as part of the procurement lifecycle. In the end, some customers are even willing to select a supplier that did not submit the cheapest bid if the supplier brings a broad range of other benefits to the relationship.

At the core, more customers now see increased access to specialist resources, the ability to enhance the services beyond those currently being provided, and the opportunity to transform the delivery of services through innovative solutions as being more important than merely reducing the cost of service delivery. To realize this, the trend tends to be away from large-scale deals involving the outsourcing of an entire organization or component of the organization toward more focused deals involving the outsourcing of business functions that are perceived as providing the best opportunity for realizing the broad range of potential benefits.

New Approach To Deals

This change in focus, and its concentration on broader parameters, is changing the fundamental approach to contracting for services. Under the traditional outsourcing approach, a customer—either on its own or in conjunction with consultants—would issue a detailed request for proposal (RFP) specifying the requirements of the customer for the services to be provided. Not only would an RFP document set the detailed requirements of the customer, it would often include voluminous documentation on the current method of providing the services and the customer's expectations with respect to the receipt of the services on an ongoing basis, with this latter component often based on some external third party's assessment of what, at that point in time, reflected their view of best of breed in the applicable industry. As structured, the entire sourcing process was intended to enable an apples-to-apples comparison of each bid and to enable a simple process of scoring each bid. As a result, a supplier was largely discouraged from bidding on the basis of a solution that deviated from the requirements or that included additional and beneficial features that added cost, as to do so would result in a lower overall score when compared with other so-called "compliant" bids. Additionally, suppliers often needed to modify their standard approach to comply with the detailed requirements specified by a customer, often resulting in significant additional cost or performance burdens that might have been avoided if the supplier's standard go-to-market approach was adopted.

In response to the shortcomings of such an approach, customers looking for more innovative solutions are moving away from the prescriptive, process-driven RFP toward an approach that is less formulaic and structured and more free form, at least at a solution level (as opposed to a legal terms level). In this respect, customers are focusing less on the process and more on getting a solution that provides—from the customer's point of view—the best approach.

In this evolving model, customers are looking to each supplier to define a best of breed solution based on the customer's list of mandatory parameters and defined business requirements. In this regard, suppliers are being challenged to offer truly innovative solutions to meet the customer's requirements and business objectives, while leveraging the supplier's standard building blocks. Using this approach, a customer can gain up-front performance and price benefits, as these are no longer subject to a supplier's ability to optimize the processes adopted internally. Further, a standardized solution—whether from a technology or operations perspective—provides greater flexibility in changing solutions or updating to new technology as it becomes available and is adopted, and is often seen as outweighing the need to adjust an organization's own tailored approach. Many customers are then redeploying these cost savings to drive further innovation or redeploying this capital to drive technology innovations within their core business. While there were initial concerns that such standardization could have a negative impact, many customers have come to recognize that, at least with respect to internal functions, the cost of maintaining customer features and functionality often outweighs the benefits of a tailored approach.

From a deal perspective, and as a result of this new approach, customers are able to push deals to market more quickly. Unlike with the old request for proposal approach, customers no longer need to invest significant time and effort in a complicated assessment on the state of their environment to determine the minutiae of the requirements, best of breed, and any deviations, before finally releasing a set of RFP documents to market. Instead, a customer can, using a core group of solution experts (often a team of subject matter experts and lawyers), develop the objectives of the customer and the high-level parameters, which can be used to solicit responses from a range of suppliers with expertise to provide the services. The trend is then to work with the preferred supplier or suppliers to develop a more detailed solution that appropriately addresses all of the customer's touch points.

While this evolving approach has significantly modified the initial approach to doing deals, it has not done away with the need to properly document the business deal. The basic requirement that the contractual document specify with certainty all of the key agreements between the parties remains, although what this really requires is determined by the nature of the deal and the specific circumstances of the transaction. While detailed statements of work may not be prepared and distributed up front, the preference is still to include a draft set of legal and business terms specifying the customer's approach to risk, pricing, and other issues. With the exception of deals that are solely cloud-based, the basic starting point is still to use the customer's paper. The benefit of this approach is that both parties are working within a known risk framework, thus avoiding any unnecessary surprises during the negotiation phase. The result is that more often than not, the legal terms and key risk allocations are often completed relatively early in the negotiation phase (with the exception of a couple of sticky issues), and much of this phase is then dedicated to the preparation and finalization of the necessary documents to reflect the overall agreement on the solution and other business terms.

Of course, the approach is often significantly different where the focus is cloud or cloud-like service. In this case, the relative inflexibility of cloud providers—based on the very standardized and utility nature of the services, the current limited number of real players in a particular space, and the limited number of cost-effective alternatives—has resulted in many of the deals involving public cloud services being negotiated using supplier paper as a starting point. Given these factors, many cloud providers are pushing a "take it or leave it" approach to negotiation to maintain strict compliance with a consistent utility model, although some seem willing to take on greater risk if the circumstances require. Further, many cloud services are initially only available through click-wrap agreements, with which the customer has almost no opportunity to negotiate or conduct due diligence. When a customer purchases cloud services, they are effectively purchasing the service "as is." This may be particularly troubling for some customers (or internal counsel at a minimum), given how easy it is to sign up for such services, and given that courts have held that click-wrap agreements are generally enforceable if there has been an explicit acceptance of the agreement by the user (for example, by clicking "I accept" before using the software).

While cloud deals can present challenges for customers who are used to doing deals on their paper, the limited nature of some of the services, the upside of utility-based pricing (discussed in more detail later in this chapter), and the upside of some inflexibility, are seen as very positive attributes and continue to drive customers to cloud-based services. In fact, some customers see the relative inflexibility of cloud-based services as a key attribute that assists in reining in the constant desire to customize or tailor licensed software beyond the available configurations to meet the desires of individual business units.

Pricing: Financial Models

Although there are many ways of paying for managed services, the most common are volume-based pricing and resource-based pricing. In certain circumstances, fixed fees may be agreed to for managed services, primarily around routine application maintenance and enhancements, where scope can be clearly defined. In such circumstances, the agreement will also include mechanisms to adjust the fixed fee to reflect changes in the applications, prioritizations, and other factors.

Volume-based pricing is primarily used for services that can be easily unitized (for example, calls to a service desk, number of end users, or number of supported devices) and where such units can be aligned with cost drivers. Volume-based pricing commonly involves the payment of a fixed price for a set volume of units, which is then adjusted to reflect any fluctuation in the consumption of services, as reflected by a count of the units during the defined period. If consumption is less than the baseline volume, then the customer receives a unitised credit. If consumption is greater, then the customer pays an additional unitised charge.

Resource-based pricing uses the number and type of individual resources (or people) assigned to provide the services as the way to calculate the charges. These resources are charged based on either full-time people (named resources) or full-time equivalents (a pool of resources). This model is most commonly seen in business process and similar sorts of process-based transactions, where it can be harder to align unitized transactions against drivers in work. Resource-based pricing models often require the customer to manage the available resources or forecast their usage, and therefore can carry the risk of idle resources.

In most instances, the pricing models will also facilitate project-based work (work that is outside day-to-day services), by establishing a set of rates and a mechanism for scoping the project-based work. To provide some protection against cost overruns, customers often include a mechanism for capping or fixing the price. As a result, there tends to be more time invested during negotiations to tie all of the documents together to reflect a cohesive explanation of the services. More so than in the template-based RFP approach, there is a need to have available resources capable of pulling together the vast array of different documents into the final cohesive set of contract documents.

Perhaps the biggest advance in pricing methodologies for managed services has been the better alignment of pricing models with the provision of the services. In this respect, many financial models are now structured around the principle of paying for services when consumed and avoiding the need to make up-front investments in equipment and software in anticipation of future demand (thus incurring costs in advance of usage). In particular, this facilitates greater cost accountability within the business at a business unit or more granular cost-center level. In this regard, cloud-based solutions reflect just the most public manifestation of a continuing trend away from building and managing information technology infrastructure (where this is not a part of the core business) toward third-party utility-based solutions that can be consumed on demand.

In large part, much of this cost model has derived from general advances in technology, including virtualization and thin provisioning, which permit the deployment of virtual assets without the need to also procure the underlying physical assets. The greater flexibility to consume resources on an as-needed basis has only continued the trend away from investment-based deals and toward a greater alignment of cost with actual spend. With the continuing move to more targeted deals with utility-based services and pricing, pricing models are less likely to include some form of minimum-spend commitment. Clearly, from an organizational perspective (and the chief financial officer, in particular), the ability to deploy capital against revenue-generating activities rather than deploying it for future internal requirements is appealing. We see the financial flexibility driven by the consumption model as a continuing and growing driver for cloud services, although this will continue to be balanced against an organization's tolerance for risk, particularly in the data security space.

Compliance with Laws: Regulatory

It should not be controversial for customers to insist that both the customer and the supplier agree to comply with all laws applicable to an outsourcing transaction, including, in the case of the supplier, those laws applicable to the performance of the services. Moreover, the solution provided by the supplier should not operate or perform in a way that would result in a customer being in breach of the obligations imposed by law.

This situation becomes more complex when dealing with changes in those laws, and specifically the question of who bears the financial responsibility for modifying the solution to ensure ongoing compliance. In the past, some suppliers have managed to turn changes in laws into a profit center, charging each customer to modify the systems to address a change in law, despite the fact that the underlying platform was common to all customers. Many suppliers will now willingly concede that such conduct would not be within the spirit of partnership and that any model that makes the customer responsible for all other changes does not always accurately reflect the most appropriate allocation of responsibility for changes in laws.

A more balanced approach is that where a law applies to the business of a party, and that law affects the services, then the relevant party should be responsible for the cost of any changes to the services that result from a change in that law. In the case of outsourcing laws, these are generally seen as the supplier's responsibility, given that a core component of the supplier's business is outsourcing. In this respect, it would seem that the supplier is best placed to lobby against such laws and adopt mitigation strategies in the event that such laws are ultimately enacted. To the extent that the supplier is unwilling to assume this responsibility, it becomes the customer's responsibility to monitor such changes and to engage, whether individually or through representative bodies, in lobbying to minimize any negative impact that could result from such changes. While the category of outsourcing laws is limited, there continues to be ongoing focus on outsourcing, and offshoring in particular in the current economic climate. Most recently, there have been a number of proposals to reform nonimmigrant visa programs.[1] One specific proposal would introduce an annual H-1B visa cap, raise H-1B wage requirements, require employers to make significant efforts to recruit US workers, and place significant outplacement restrictions on certain companies (primarily companies considered to be using the nonimmigrant visa programs as a source of cheap labor).

Data Security: Privacy

Data security and individual privacy have become a major focus of most sourcing transactions as successful attacks of customer systems and networks become more common. For instance, in its *2013 Cost of Cyber Crime Study: Global* report, the Ponemon Institute found that companies that were the

---

[1] *See* Border Security, Economic Opportunity, and Immigration Modernization Act, S. 744, 113th Cong. (2013) (also known as the Immigration Act).

subject of the study experienced 343 successful attacks a week.[2] A successful attack was defined in the study as one that resulted in the infiltration of the company's core networks or enterprise systems, not including attacks stopped by the company's firewall defenses. According to the study, the results represented 1.4 successful attacks per company per week.

There is no general statutory framework for privacy laws in the United States. Certain federal regulations apply to financial institutions, health care information, and the protection of children's privacy online. Also, the Federal Trade Commission has become a *de facto* federal privacy regulator through a broad interpretation of its mandate to protect consumers. Almost every state has adopted laws that require certain standards of protection and security, including requirements that companies notify affected individuals when personal information has been subject to unauthorized access or use. The circumstances that require disclosure, and the nature of the disclosure, vary from state to state. In some cases, money damages can be recoverable as a result of a failure to comply. In Europe, the Data Protection Directive currently provides a framework for privacy, data security, and the transfer of information.[3] In particular, it provides restrictions on transfers to jurisdictions that do not provide adequate protection. Unfortunately, many member states have implemented the directive inconsistently, resulting in significant complexity and administrative burden in ensuring compliance. In response, the European Commission has been working on a regulatory framework to replace the directive and the data protection laws of each member state (although it will not impact other laws that may impact data privacy, such as employment laws), creating a single set of data protection laws within the European Economic Area. The new regulation is intended to strengthen and make prescriptive the key principles set out in the directive. For instance, the regulation will expand upon the directives' requirement to implement appropriate organizational and security measures to protect data by requiring that such measures ensure a level of security appropriate to the risks represented by the processing and the nature of the personal data to be protected. Such an approach requires a specific review of the risks with respect to each category of data and each processing activity and will ultimately require a layered approach to security and privacy, depending on the outcome of these risk reviews.

---

[2] Ponemon Institute, *2013 Fourth Annual Cost of Cyber Crime Study: Global* (2013).
[3] Directive 95/46/EC.

Given the patchwork of regulatory requirements in the United States and globally, it is left to each customer to define its own requirements for privacy and security based on the types of data being shared with the supplier, the applicable regulatory framework, and the risks associated with the processing and potential compromise or loss of that data. In a traditional outsourcing context, most suppliers will commit to implement security measures to protect customer data as well as agree to notify a customer of a breach or potential breach. Generally, a supplier's obligations with respect to data security and privacy in this context will tie to the greater of the applicable industry standards, including ISO 27001 (Information technology—Security techniques—Information security management systems—Requirements), ISO 27002 (Information technology—Security techniques—Code of practice for information security management), the customer's policy, and laws applicable to the handling, transportation and use of customer data. Additionally, suppliers will often agree to complete an annual audit of their compliance with the controls related to data security and privacy. Depending on whether financial data is involved, such an audit will either be completed pursuant to AICPA guidelines for reporting on service organization controls (SOC) and in conformance with AICPA standard section AT101 (where no financial data is held and the only requirement is for a SOC 2 Type II report addressing security, availability, processing integrity, confidentiality, and privacy) or International Standard on Assurance Engagements No. 3402 and the Statement on Standards Attestation Engagements No. 16 (where financial data is held and the requirement is for a SOC 2 Type II report addressing financial controls as well as security, availability, processing integrity, confidentiality, and privacy).

As most cloud deals are, for now, documented on supplier paper, there is a wide variety of potential contractual provisions and outcomes. In this respect, it is possible that the starting point will not include some of the most basic of protections, including details on the types of information retained, clarity on the customer's ownership of the data stored on or generated through the use of the cloud service, prohibition on the use or sale (whether in aggregate and de-identified form or not) of customer data (some cloud contracts will expressly permit the provider to use and commercialize customer data), limitations on the regions within which data must reside, and a clear right of return of customer data upon the termination or expiration of the agreement. The absence of basic terms and appropriate frameworks for data security and privacy means that more effort may be required to validate the acceptability of a cloud solution. To some extent, the lack of legal framework may not be fatal to the adoption of a cloud solution, particularly if the risks involved can be mitigated in other ways. In this case, some cloud providers are as willing as traditional outsourcers to provide regular reports on applicable controls (similar to those discussed earlier), although the utility of this may be limited depending on how the cloud service is structured. For instance, many cloud services will reflect the multi-layered approach that is becoming common within the industry, with a cloud service itself being a consumer of cloud services (e.g., software made available on the cloud is resident on cloud-based infrastructure and storage), which makes it challenging to physically assess the risk within each layer. The ability to assess the security risk posed by cloud services in this instance can be further complicated if the security organization is more familiar with assessing security risk in an insourced or traditional outsourced environment where there is, to some degree, an ability to see the physical objects being protected and to validate, at least from a physical perspective, the protections that have been implemented. Despite these initial hurdles, customers have been able to include cloud-based services within their environment after conducting an assessment of the actual risk posed by the particular solution and then negotiating appropriate adjustments to the legal framework and implementing valid business and technical work-arounds.

Further, the proposed new data privacy regulation in Europe (as previously discussed) will potentially complicate the provision of and use of cloud services in their current form. Importantly, the proposed regulation will require customers to ensure that any supplier utilized by the customer complies with the regulation, including cloud suppliers. Practically, this would require cloud providers to implement mechanisms for identifying data subject to the regulation so that it can be treated differently from other data (such different treatment may include storage and processing of regulated data within the European Union). Such an approach is apt to create problems for cloud providers (and other providers of utility-based systems and services) who routinely argue that customers should be more concerned with the relevant functionality and performance of the service and less with the detail of how it is constructed, operated, and managed. In this respect, the position of cloud providers remains consistent with the differentiation they draw between cloud and traditional managed services—that a customer of cloud services is purchasing functionality, which, unlike a more traditional managed service, does not include any say in how that functionality is delivered. If a customer is more concerned with the manner in which that functionality is provided, then cloud services may not be appropriate. It would appear from a regulatory perspective that the European Commission does not agree with the view that a customer should not be concerned with the manner of performance, something that will likely have profound implications for how cloud services are delivered in the future.

Risk Allocation and Liability Limits

Each contractual relationship has at its core a number of objectives, on the one hand documenting the business deal (or transaction) and on the other hand allocating risk between the parties. The time taken to consider and allocate risk reflects that there is, in the end, no such thing as a "risk-free" transaction, and that even a low-risk transaction at the outset may come to include higher-risk items (or risk may be elevated due to changes or a better understanding of the issues). It also reflects that, fundamentally, and despite any outsourcing, the operational risk always resides with the customer. As a result, the allocation of risk, whether operational, financial, or legal, is ultimately the final backstop in the event that the parties are unable to use governance to produce a positive outcome for both.

From a practical, service delivery perspective, the contractual documentation is about setting out the scope, price, and level of service. In so doing, however, the contact also achieves one of its core objectives, the allocation of risk. By setting out the responsibility of the supplier and the customer, the contract explicitly allocates the risk for performance and non-performance of those assigned tasks. Namely, the supplier is rewarded for its proper performance of the allocated tasks by the payment of fees, but has at risk reduced payment if the level of performance is below what is contracted (or is at risk of non-payment in certain cases, for issues such as non-performance). Beyond this allocation of responsibility and risk, the contractual framework manages contractual and other risks through a variety of other mechanisms, including warranties, indemnities, and liability caps.

It is now common for outsourcing agreements to include some form of cap with respect to a customer's direct losses arising from a supplier's non-performance of the services (that is, losses that arise from operational issues). While this could result in a customer bearing some of the risk of a supplier's non-performance to the extent that losses exceed the agreed-to cap, it is unrealistic to expect that the outsourcing of services would absolve the customer of all of the risks associated with the delivery of the services, particularly as a customer would be solely responsible in an insourced environment. In addition, transactions will include a limited waiver of indirect damages such as consequential losses and lost profits.

The cap for direct damages is typically an aggregate cap over the term of the agreement, specified as a fixed amount or a multiple of the amounts payable under the agreement. Where the cap is a multiple of the amounts payable under the agreement, it is becoming more common to specify an amount as a floor. Typically, the cap is agreement-wide, and is not partitioned by statement of work or in any other way, with the limited exception of some additional larger caps for certain items, as discussed later in this chapter.

Outside of the actual direct damages cap, the real issue these days is what losses are subject to the direct damages cap. Typically, the objective of the direct damages cap is to provide a supplier with certainty regarding its exposure for operational issues (that is, failure to deliver the specified services in accordance with the requirements set forth in the agreement). The usual approach is then to carve out failures that are not operational in nature (such as confidentiality, intellectual property breaches, etc.) as well as indemnities and breaches attributable to "bad acts" such as gross negligence or fraud. In the cases of these failures, each party is expected to take full responsibility for the losses that arise (that is, these should be uncapped). In this instance, particular categories of damages are often carved out of both the direct damages cap and the waiver of consequential damages.

Many of these exclusions are non-controversial, due primarily to the fact that they apply mutually to both the supplier and customer. One area, however, that continues to evolve is the nature of any liability exclusion for privacy and data security breaches. There is really a vast range of potential outcomes in this regard, with a large number of factors ultimately determining where this lands. However, it is clear that suppliers are taking increasingly aggressive stances on liability for data security and privacy breaches in light of the increasing number of high-profile breaches/losses and an increasingly complex regulatory framework. It is probably fair to say that, at this stage, this is often one of the last issues to be resolved by the parties and often involves the striking of some compromise, which results in the customer sharing some amount of acceptable risk.

Some suppliers continue to request that credits, including service level credits, and in some instances certain damages be specified as the sole and exclusive remedy. It is uncommon that this would be agreed to in a contract as it limits a customer's ability to recover its actual losses related to a performance failure of the supplier, and service level credits are rarely established based on the losses to be suffered by the customer. Further, such a provision has, among other things, the effect of imposing a secondary and lower cap on a supplier's liability for non-performance in areas identified by the customer, which is already adequately addressed as part of the overall cap on direct damages. Additionally, such a limitation would preclude the customer from exercising any available termination rights, including a right to terminate for breach. That said, it is common for the outsourcing agreement to provide that any service level credits paid will offset any future damages award.

Governance

As the market moves away from large-scale sole-sourced deals toward more targeted deals and multi-supplier environments and a greater use of cloud, governance, and the management of contractual arrangements is becoming a much more of a fundamental part of an organization's toolkit. In this regard, the terms of the contractual relationship provide the framework within which the agreement is governed and also provides the levers that can be used to incent performance. As the complexity of the contractual relationships expands to reflect the complexity of the systems and services and the ability to actually physically fix problems, there is a greater need for strong management and governance skills (in addition to a detailed understanding of the technology).

At this stage, the trend appears to be toward a metric-focused form of governance, with suppliers being measured not only against their performance of the services but also against defined governance metrics, such as timely provision of reports. In some cases, the ramifications of a failure to comply will be the same irrespective of whether it is a failure to perform the services or a failure to comply with a governance requirement. In some instances, this detailed approach to governance has devolved into an unbalanced approach, whereby every deliverable and obligation within a contract is recorded and then tracked on a monthly basis, often without any view as to the relative importance of the obligation or its impact on the business deal. Unfortunately, this data-driven approach is often coupled with a rigid and inflexible view of contractual performance, which requires the supplier to earn its partnership status by jumping through an ever-expanding set of hoops. In this case, rather than acknowledging that circumstances may change or that issues may present themselves that were not evident during the contracting process that should, in the interests of fair and equitable treatment, result in adjustments to the contractual framework, the data-driven and inflexible approach insists on strict contractual compliance, irrespective of the benefits of that approach or any alternative approach. In the end, governance in this form often fails to align the performance of the supplier with the customer's broader objective, namely the success of the business through the generation of revenue and profit.

To more accurately focus the agreement (and governance) on the key fundamentals of a deal, some customers have reoriented their approach to governance and service levels to focus on those issues that are core to the customer's business. In this case, rather than measuring minutia of a deal (such as speed-to-answer, support performance, executive support performance, reporting compliance) the service levels focus on those core revenue generating aspects of the customer's business and attach a significant service level credit to any failure related to this. There are two key challenges with this approach, firstly, accepting that certain failures that could attract the wrath of senior executives are to be managed through a process outside of a service level credit. This can be a significant challenge where the team putting together the contract will ultimately have to defend the focus of the service level credits. Secondly, for some organizations, defining what is fundamental (or the most important) aspect of their business can be challenging. For instance, with an airline, is taking an online ticket reservation of lesser, greater, or equal importance than printing boarding passes and dispatching planes? The key to resolving this challenge is to understand the concerns of senior executives with respect to the day-to-day operation of the business and then have these ranked in terms of level of importance. In most instances, the focus tends to be on areas that are likely to result in lost revenue, material compensation costs or significant reputational damage rather than on a days' worth of back office productivity or lost e-mail, as disruptive and embarrassing as that might be.

In the end, every relationship has its challenges, and each participant in the relationship has its strengths and weaknesses that need to be balanced to achieve the goals of the participants. Governance is really about understanding the relative strengths and weaknesses of each participant and managing the relationship to get the best possible outcome for the customer. While data is an essential element of this, a very rigid and process-oriented approach can limit the ability of the governance team to see the real problems and the creative solutions that may be taken to address those problems. Predictably, it is all about striking the right balance between flexibility and contractual compliance. Too much flexibility, and the supplier may under deliver, not enough flexibility and mutual opportunities may be missed.

Conclusion

It is clear that the approach to deals and the nature of the solution is changing and evolving, with a distinct shift from large single supplier deals to more focused deals aimed at driving a broad range of benefits for the customer. Yet, it is equally clear that no single solution works for every customer and the best, or most appropriate model, is only likely to be determined after a proper consideration of all of the relevant facts and circumstances. The trend among customers is to adopt processes and solutions that drive future benefits for the company (rather than groups) in light of the overall business direction. Groups that previously were focused on solving their problems or issues are now being challenged to put forward solutions to business problems and issues, and as such, it is no longer possible for the overall objectives of the broader business to be marginalized when looking at sourcing transactions.

As the landscape evolves it is clear that this new approach will provide new challenges to how business is done and the processes that may be adopted to compare offerings from different suppliers. While models that result in the objective comparison of suppliers based on allocated scores and weightings will continue to have their place in the sourcing environment, these models will need to be carefully balanced with the need for innovative solutions that enable each supplier to present their best model in response to any initiative. As the analysis trends away from cost reductions and the necessary financial imperative, such models will need to adapt to answer the broader question of what solution drives the best future benefit for the organization as a whole—whether this is freeing capital or people to focus on the core functions of the organization or obtaining access to scarce resources who can provide knowledge and expertise that might not otherwise be available to an organization.

Key Takeaways

- Before starting a sourcing initiative there needs to be clarity at all levels as to the business objectives and tolerance for risk. Both objectives and risk tolerance should consider the benefits and risks to the entire organization and not just focus on the immediate needs of a particular business unit. This should also include decisions regarding approach to sourcing (is it customer driven or solution driven) and technologies (cloud, utility, etc.).

- Executive engagement is important—both within the relevant business unit, but also across the organization. Many of the key decisions on approach, solution, and risk should be socialized to a broad group of stakeholders to avoid future questions about the process.

- To the extent possible the customer should dictate the starting point for legal terms and conditions (noting, that currently this may not be practical for cloud solutions) to ensure a fair and balanced starting position.

- Early and practical engagement with legal counsel is highly desirable in developing both the strategy and the tactical approach to sourcing. As the landscape changes legal counsel are often in the best position to provide guidance on new approaches and adjustments to standard playbooks to put in place a favorable relationship.

- The sourcing process, and governance, should not be structured as an adversarial process. While the different perspectives have to be respected the process and the relationship should be about mutual benefit for all concerned—differences of opinion and perspective need to be discussed to see if a "partnership" balance can be struck between the parties.

- The deal should be considered holistically and not just from a single angle. The relationship between scope, performance and price and the impact of risk need to be viewed together to understand the overall nature of the deal and whether, in the end, it is beneficial for the customer.

Daniel R. Mummery is a partner with Gibson Dunn & Crutcher. His practice encompasses a wide range of technology transactions and sourcing matters, with a particular emphasis on complex on-shore and offshore information technology and business process outsourcing transactions, including outsourcing renegotiations and restructurings, shared services, business transformation, licensing, and contract manufacturing arrangements. His ITO experience includes infrastructure, ADM, IT security, end-user computing, help desk, call center, and managed network transactions. His BPO experience includes HR, finance and accounting, procurement and supply chain management, claims processing, facilities management, clinical programs, fulfillment, and logistics transactions. Mr. Mummery has worked with a broad range of clients in major sourcing engagements and technology transaction matters, including some of the largest automotive, communications, energy, financial services, health care, manufacturing, media, technology and transportation companies in the world, as well as emerging growth companies and private equity and venture capital investors. He has represented such clients as American Express, AT&T, BellSouth, British Telecommunications, Cable & Wireless, Charles Schwab, Chevron, Clorox Company, Continental Airlines, Conway, DuPont, Gateway, General Motors, KPMG, Levi Strauss & Co., McGraw-Hill, Miller Brewing Company, NetApp, Ryder, Symantec, Tenet Health care, and United Air Lines.

Mr. Mummery is ranked by Chambers & Partners *as one of the very best outsourcing lawyers in the world.* Chambers USA Guide (2013) *and* Chambers Global Guide (2013) *have awarded him their highest rankings in the categories of Outsourcing (USA, Band 1), IT Outsourcing (California, Star Individual) and Outsourcing (Nationwide, Band 1). According to* Chambers, *Mr. Mummery is "a recognized authority in the field" who "fiercely protects client interests and provides high-value, strategic business and legal advice." Mr. Mummery is also included in Practical Law Company's* Cross-border Outsourcing Handbook *(2011-2012),* The Best Lawyers in America 2013, The Lawdragon 500 (New Stars, New Worlds),

Global Counsel 3000, *and* Mondaq Business Briefing, Survey of Leading E-Commerce Lawyers *and is a member of the Advisory Board of* Global E-Commerce Law and Business Report. *He has been recognized as a Leading Lawyer in the* Legal 500 US (Media, Technology & Telecoms, Technology – Outsourcing) *for his outstanding outsourcing and technology transactions practice for many years. Mr. Mummery's work in structuring, negotiating, and implementing outsourcing transactions has been featured in* The Recorder, The Daily Deal, *and* Business Finance. *He is a frequent lecturer on outsourcing topics including, most recently, at ITO, BPO and offshoring programs organized by* BusinessWeek, *Gartner, Sourcing Interests Group and The Conference Board.*

Acknowledgment: *The author gratefully acknowledges the contributions of Alex Claringbould and Britten Westsmith, Gibson Dunn & Crutcher associates and members of the firm's Strategic Sourcing and Technology Transactions Practice Group, in the conception, development, and preparation of this chapter.*

Adapting a Service Level Agreement to Technology

Jon Grossman

Partner

Dickstein Shapiro LLP

ASPATORE

Introduction

A service level agreement (SLA) is an agreement between a customer and a service provider, wherein the service provider agrees to furnish a cost-effective and reliable service to the customer. These agreements are important to ensure effective outsourcing relationships and long-term success because they define the customer's expectations and outline the service provider's performance criteria up front, alleviating confusion and specifying remedies should disputes arise. This chapter examines the different considerations that should be addressed when structuring a SLA. A SLA should first and foremost specify the legal obligations of the service provider and the service recipient as well as the technical requirements of the project. It should also have sections detailing pricing, privacy, security, intellectual property ownership, and risk mitigation. This chapter also discusses key content areas of a SLA. It focuses on the assigned functions of a service provider, specifically examining the levels of measurement and legal issues related to different functions. The chapter also analyzes the impact technology has had on service level agreements, looking at a customer's encryption requirements to the service provider's use of a multi-tenant cloud environment to process and store customers' data. The chapter concludes by emphasizing that SLAs should be adaptable to reflect changes in market conditions, business requirements, and technology.

Structuring Service Level Agreements

A service level agreement is designed to stipulate specific performance criteria that the outsourcing provider must meet. By definition, an SLA must therefore reflect the legal obligations of the service provider and service recipient as well as the technical requirements of the project. The SLA needs to address legal issues such as pricing and consequences for poor performance. The technical section should define service levels that reflect both the recipient's business needs and the technical realities and constraints imposed on the parties. For example, the SLA should specify the levels of availability, performance criteria, security, and any other features of the service. A service provider may enter into numerous SLAs, each with a different client, or multiple SLAs with a single client providing different services under each agreement. A client may also enter into multiple SLAs with different service providers.

Legal Terms and Conditions of a Service Level Agreement

When structuring an outsourcing SLA, it should be written as a self-contained legal document. This is crucial for a number of reasons. First, a single document provides clarity. By defining a commonly understood framework of the customer's needs, expectations, and priorities, the SLA will help avoid and alleviate disputes. The financial arrangement between the parties and the duration of the contract should also be explicitly spelled out in the SLA.[1] In the event that issues arise with the service, neither party can plead ignorance. Furthermore, the SLA should define measurable performance criteria, or "service levels," that the service provider must meet. These service levels will provide the foundation for remedial measures and for imposing any contractual penalties, should the service provider's performance be inadequate. In most cases, contract termination will be permissible only in the event of a material breach. Second, a single document reduces the risk of incompleteness. If multiple documents are piecemealed together to create an agreement, a key section could easily be left out of the final agreement. Third, a single document is easier to reference later. Both parties will have a single source specifying their respective legal obligations and technical expectations. Fourth, a single SLA reduces the challenge of inconsistencies with similar terms and conditions contained in other documents. However, if other agreements (such as a license agreement) exist, it is necessary to have a document priority of interpretation section in the SLA. This section will specify which document is controlling to the extent that any inconsistencies exist between the two or more documents.

The technical aspects of a service level agreement are also critical. They define the scope of the SLA. The SLA should first state exactly what services the customer requires.[2] Then, it should set service levels for availability, monitoring, performance, accuracy, security, and affordability. These levels, or performance criteria, should be technically meaningful and achievable. The SLA, for example, might state that a system must be available 99.99 percent of the time except for regularly scheduled maintenance downtime.[3] It might

---

[1] See infra pp. # for a discussion of the pricing structure of a service level agreement.

[2] For example, a customer might contract with a telecommunications service provider for Internet access.

[3] No system is perfect. Therefore, demanding that a system be available 100 percent of the

also provide levels for system monitoring that range from periodic system testing to check for proper functioning to external scans performed by third-party security vendors to ensure that the customer's data remains secured. The levels outlined in the SLA do not have to reflect technical norms for the industry. The customer will use these defined levels, however, to determine whether the service provider's performance was satisfactory, above expectations, or below expectations. This in turn will serve as the foundation for the bonus-and-penalty system.[4]

There are several financial aspects to consider when entering a service level agreement. The goal of the arrangement is to provide a service to the customer, which is cost-effective and reliable. To ensure these goals are met, the SLA specifies performance criteria that the outsourcing provider must meet. The customer can use a bonus-and-penalty system to enforce the contract. If the service provider fails to meet the defined service levels, it will be penalized. Essentially, the customer will receive a credit, or a reduction in the following month's bill, because of the service provider's poor performance. On the other hand, if the service provider exceeds the performance criteria, it receives a bonus. The better the provider can service the customer, the better the customer can achieve its overall business objectives. Thus, a credit award system gives the most meaning to an SLA.

Although the contractual/legal and technical sections are the most important ones in the SLA, other considerations must be included in the document. The SLA should have sections detailing the use of computer open source software and intellectual property ownership.[5] At a minimum, most parties will want to maintain ownership of their existing intellectual property and license the technology to the other party. The SLA should specify the terms of these licenses. The SLA should additionally specify which party would own any jointly developed intellectual property. Alternatively, the parties may agree to open source development, granting universal access and a free license to any jointly developed products.

---

time is an unrealistic expectation that the service provider could not achieve.
[4] For an in-depth discussion of a bonus-and-penalty system in an SLA, see *infra* pp. #.
[5] *See infra* pp. # for a discussion of IP ownership.

Geographic considerations also factor into service level agreements. This is especially true when the service provider and customer are located in different time zones. In such a situation, the service level agreement should include a section specifying the service provider's hours, ensuring it is available, at a minimum, during the customer's business hours. The geographic location of the service provider or the customer may also affect which laws govern the agreement. As a result, the parties may choose to insert a choice of law provision into the SLA, electing the laws of a certain state to govern any disputes arising under the agreement. Lastly, if the service provider's servers are located outside of the United States, any data transmitted to and from them may be subject to export control regulations.

Privacy is also a consideration that an SLA needs to address. The SLA should specify which privacy laws govern. Privacy laws can differ in both terms of context and locale. For example, if the customer is going to have the service provider process, transmit, or store health information of individuals, then the Health Insurance Portability and Accountability Act will govern the SLA's privacy terms.[6] When the SLA involves legally protected data, the service provider must be able to prove its compliance with the applicable law or regulations.[7] A service provider must also comply with privacy settings and policies of a social media platform if interaction with or management of such a platform is required under the SLA.[8] Privacy laws also differ for US-based and European-based service providers and customers.

Key Content Areas of a Service Level Agreement

Functions of a Service Provider

To fulfill its obligations under the SLA, the service provider will have assigned functions that it must meet. Certain functions will require different measurement levels. Levels of measurement, for example, can be based on

---

[6] 42 U.S.C. § 1306 (West).

[7] *See infra* pp. #.

[8] For example, a customer might hire a service provider to act as its social media representative. The SLA should dictate the terms regarding tweeting, posting, and blogging. The service provider will not only be required to follow these terms, but it must also abide by the privacy policies of the different social media platforms, such as Facebook, Twitter, and Pinterest.

volume output or speed. The availability of the system/host will be judged based on time and agreed-upon targets. As stated earlier, the SLA may require that the system be available 99.99 percent of the time except for regularly scheduled maintenance downtime. If the service provider fails to satisfy this benchmark, the customer can enforce a contractual penalty. Additionally, the service provider should be available, at a minimum, during the customer's normal business hours.

Alternatively, the response time of the help desk will be judged based on speed. The SLA should specify how much time the service provider has to respond upon the customer's notification that a problem exists with the service. The response time usually varies with the severity of the problem. For example, if it is a "Level 1" problem, meaning the problem causes a complete loss of service to the customer, the service provider must respond to the client within thirty minutes of notification 100 percent of the time. However, if the problem is a "Level 4" issue, meaning it causes no loss of service and in no way impedes the use of the system, the service provider may respond to the client within three working days of notification 100 percent of the time. The SLA should also include escalation procedures in the event the service provider's response and resolution of the problem are unsatisfactory.

In a transaction system, performance will be judged based on volume output. For instance, a customer may outsource its credit card processing to a service provider. In the SLA, the customer will require that service provider be able to process, for example, up to ten credit card transactions per second. If the service provider fails to meet this benchmark, the customer can impose a contractual penalty.

Certain functions will also trigger different legal issues. If the function requires that the parties exchange confidential information, the SLA should include provisions about the protection and use of such information both during the duration of agreement and upon its termination. The SLA should also specify how the service provider should respond if it is compelled by the government or by the courts to disclose the customer's confidential information or personal data. To the extent that it is practical and permissible by law, the service provider should notify the customer as soon as it receives such a request and cooperate with the customer's efforts to manage the release of such data. The customer should follow the same procedure if compelled to disclose the service provider's confidential information.

Privacy concerns also trigger legal issues. There are several federal statutes that establish privacy rights.[9] Namely, by law, certain types of information must be protected. If a customer requires a service provider to process, store, or transmit protected information, it must be documented in the SLA. The SLA should therefore outline the customer's requirements for data encryption, retention, and deletion, including its expectations of the service provider for returning and destroying the customer's personal data upon termination of the service. It should state how the service provider would prove that it complied with the retention and deletion requirements. This will require a certain level of transparency on the service provider's part.

Security concerns also pose a problem. Encryption is therefore a critical requirement for securing data. The SLA should detail how the service provider will protect the data, preventing it not only from being disclosed either accidently or deliberately but also preventing it from being corrupted. It should specify the encryption algorithms used to protect the customer's data both while it is in transit and while it is in storage. Typically, the service provider holds the encryption key. However, given today's privacy concerns, some vendors are now giving the keys to customers because it requires the government to ask the customers for access to their data instead of secretly forcing the service provider's hand.[10]

Pricing Structure of a Service Level Agreement

The pricing structure within a service level agreement should be defined with sufficient detail because the structure can often be complex depending on the number of services provided, the customization of the service required, and the required availability of the service provider. First, the

---

[9] *See, e.g.,* Health Insurance Portability and Accountability Act 42 U.S.C. § 1306 (West); Fair Credit Reporting Act, 15 U.S.C. §§ 1681-1681u (2012); Gramm-Leach-Bliley Act, 15 U.S.C. §§ 6801-6809 (2012).

[10] Jaikumar Vijayan, *Cloud computing 2014: Moving to a zero-trust security model,* COMPUTER WORLD (Dec. 31, 2013), *http://www.computerworld.com/s/article/9244959/Cloud_computing_ 2014_Moving_to_a_zero_trust_security_model?taxonomyId=84&pageNumber=1.*

pricing structure should differentiate routine services from custom ones. If the customer requires only routine services that the service provider provides regularly, the cost should be lower as compared to a customer who requires custom services. Second, the pricing should also vary depending on the level of care offered. If the customer requires on-site support, that level should evidence an upward adjustment of the cost. An on-site service provider will be focused exclusively on the one customer and will be easily accessible. The customer should be required to pay for these premium benefits. However, if the customer can be adequately supported via a remote site, the pricing should be lowered. The pricing structure should also differentiate between customers requiring the service provider to be available twenty-four hours a day, seven days a week as opposed to those customers only requiring support during regular business hours. Third, the more services the customers require, the higher the cost of the contract. Fourth, the SLA should specify additional expenses such as third-party assistance and travel that the customer is expected to bear as well as the process around submitting and approving for those costs.

The pricing structure can also be used to enforce the contract by setting up a bonus-and-penalty system. In such a system, the service provider will be contractually penalized if it fails to meet the performance criteria outlined in the SLA. The contractual penalty can be a stipulated amount or it can be based on a percentage of the service fees. The reduction may be set up on a sliding scale, giving the customer a larger discount based on the magnitude of the service provider's breach. For example, the amount a customer is required to pay will be reduced in direct proportion to the amount of time the service is unavailable. If the service provider, on the other hand, exceeds the specified criteria, it will receive additional compensation. A bonus-and-penalty system not only ensures that the service provider meets the outlined performance criteria, but gives the service provider incentive for going above and beyond the call of the SLA. Furthermore, it attaches consequences to a service provider's failure to meet the outlined performance criteria and gives the customer the ability to penalize the service provider without requiring the customer to terminate the contract.

The frequency and type of payments should also be incorporated in the pricing structure of the SLA. It should define whether payments are due up front, whether they should be paid monthly, or whether they should be paid upon the achievement of certain milestones. A tension exists between these methods. Service providers would prefer to receive compensation up-front because it will generate cash flow and guarantee payment. Customers, conversely, would prefer to make monthly or milestone payments based on progress, ensuring they only pay for the services actually received. Regardless of the method of payment selected, it should be defined clearly in the SLA to avoid future conflict. The SLA should also stipulate that the customer must pay within, for instance, thirty days upon the receipt of an invoice. It should then stipulate any consequences for late payment, such as allowing the service provider to charge interest on overdue payments or suspend service.

Ownership of Intellectual Property

The intellectual property rights of each party should be detailed in the SLA. Intellectual property rights are usually balanced between the parties. On the one hand, if the rights are associated with a commercial off-the-shelf product, then the service provider owns the intellectual property and licenses the technology to its customers. The service provider can offer an exclusive or non-exclusive license. Sometimes customers prefer to receive an exclusive license for their industry. For example, a law firm will enter a service level agreement with a service provider for all of its billing needs. An agreement will be reached between the parties where the service provider will agree not to offer its billing system to any other law firms. But it will have the option to license to an accounting firm or engineering company. This type of limitation is known as a "field of use" restriction. On the other hand, if the rights are associated with a custom product built in compliance with the customer's specifications, then the customer will likely want to own the intellectual property and license back the technology to the service provider.

Assigning intellectual property rights to one party or another is difficult when the product begins as commercial off-the-shelf but is then modified to fit a customer's specific needs. In such a situation, both parties have a vested interest in owning the jointly developed intellectual property. The parties can be co-owners, but this introduces a host of problems because it significantly affects each owner's ability to exercise its rights. For instance, each owner is free to assign or license the invention without the other owner's approval.[11] In other words, Owner A could license the technology to Owner B's competitors and there is nothing Owner B could do to stop it. Co-ownership requires the parties to trust one another. Additionally, a third party could negotiate with both Owner A and Owner B, pitting the parties against each other and driving the cost down, resulting in a depreciation of the value of the intellectual property rights associated with the product. Lastly, both parties must agree to bring an infringement suit, otherwise, the owner filing the complaint will lack standing.[12] Thus, it is usually better if only one party owns the jointly developed intellectual property while the other party receives, in turn, a license back that fits their needs.

Ownership of jointly developed intellectual property will be driven by economics. Likely, one party will value the intellectual property more than the other will and be willing to pay a higher price for it. If the customer wants to be the sole owner, then it will pay more under the contract. Conversely, if the service provider wants to be the sole owner, it will reduce the price of its services.

Technology Components

Information technology advances have significantly affected SLAs. Service providers often process, store, and transmit customer's personal data using cloud-computing technology. Cloud-computing technology allows users to store data externally on remote servers and allows them to access the data from anywhere via the Internet. A service provider often utilizes the same cloud technology for all of its customers, creating a multi-tenant cloud environment. Although there are many benefits associated with cloud computing technology, there are several concerns that must be addressed in an SLA.

Security and privacy are big concerns. If a customer contracts with a service provider that utilizes cloud-computing technology, the customer will have to relinquish some of its control. The service provider, rather than the customer, will be responsible for the security of the data and for auditing the system. Security concerns are heightened when data is stored on the

---

[11] 35 U.S.C. § 262 (West 2012).
[12] *See id.*; *Ethicon, Inc. v. U.S. Surgical Corp.*, 135 F.3d 1456, 1468 (Fed. Cir. 1998).

cloud. Hackers might be more tempted to attack a cloud because a successful hack means it gains the personal data of all of the service provider's customers. Encryption is therefore a critical requirement for securing data on the cloud. Furthermore, the SLA should specify how the service provider isolates data and applications if it processes or stores the customer's data in a multi-tenant cloud environment. A customer needs to be assured that its data will not be mixed with another customer's data despite being on the same server. Notwithstanding, a customer might still specify that certain categories of personal data not be sent to or processed in the cloud, such as individuals' health information.

In today's golden age of smart devices, people expect everything to be accessible at their fingertips twenty-four hours a day, seven days a week. This expectation has affected SLAs. An SLA should include a section on whether the customer can access its contracted service via a smart device. This might require the service provider to design and license an app to the customer. If the service is available on a smart device, extra security measures need to be in place. The smart device, for instance, might include a "mobile kill switch" that allows the customer to wipe the data from the device remotely if the device is stolen. The price of the SLA should account for these extras.

Risk Mitigation

As with any contract, a service level agreement should assign risk of loss and outline risk mitigation strategies. In most cases, the service provider bears the risk of loss in the event of data loss, network outages, or security breaches. This means that, depending on the severity of the failure, the customer will be entitled to a credit (i.e., a reduction on next month's bill) or it will have the right to terminate the SLA. For example, an SLA might provide that the customer is entitled to a credit for any interruption of electrical power not caused by the customer lasting one to eight hours. However, if the outage lasts eight hours or more, it will be considered a breach of a material term of the SLA, giving the customer the option to terminate the contract.

To mitigate some of the risk, the service provider may require that the SLA include a *force majeure* clause. Essentially, if the service failure is due to a war, an act of God, a strike, weather, or other uncontrollable forces, the service provider will be excused from performance standards. The service provider may also want to cap its total liability under the agreement to mitigate some of the risk. The limit can be a fixed or variable amount. To mitigate some of the risk on the customer's end, the customer may require that the service provider have a minimum level of insurance to ensure that any negligence or liabilities are financially covered. This also gives the service provider the option to cap its liability at the insurance maximum.

If the SLA includes a software license, the parties may agree to a source code escrow to mitigate the licensee's risk. Specifically, the software licensor will deposit the source code of the software with a third-party escrow agent. The agent is typically responsible for maintenance of the software. The agent will also be responsible for releasing the source code to the licensee if the licensor files for bankruptcy or otherwise breaches the software terms of the SLA.

Lastly, the SLA should contain provisions related to bankruptcy. An SLA frequently includes a clause allowing for termination of the agreement if either party becomes bankrupt or insolvent. The parties may also wish to invoke the protection offered under Section 365(n) of the bankruptcy code.[13] Namely, in the event the licensor of intellectual property goes bankrupt and rejects the license, Section 365(n) protects the licensee and allows it to retain its rights to the licensed intellectual property.[14] The licensee also has the option to terminate the contract and sue for monetary damages.[15]

Conclusion

An SLA is an agreement between a customer and a service provider, wherein the service provider provides a cost-effective and reliable service to the customer. By defining the customer's expectations and outlining the service provider's performance criteria up front, the SLA protects both parties, and should disputes arise, will alleviate confusion and specify remedies. During the term of an SLA, market conditions and business

---

[13] 11 U.S.C. § 365(n) (West 2012).
[14] *Id.*
[15] *Id.*

requirements will change and technology will advance. An SLA, therefore, needs to be adaptable. The terms of the agreement should be reviewed periodically and adjusted to reflect these changes. The pricing should also be adjusted to account for inflation. Lastly, given the current concerns over privacy and security, service providers should be amenable to incorporating the latest technology advances into their servers and networks.

Key Takeaways

- An outsourcing service level agreement should be structured as a self-contained legal document. This is crucial because it provides clarity, reduces risk of incompleteness, is easier to reference later, and eliminates inconsistencies between multiple documents.

- The technical section of a service level agreement should define service levels that reflect both the recipient's business needs and the technical realities and constraints imposed on the parties.

- A bonus-and-penalty system should be outlined in the SLA and be used to enforce the terms of the agreement. If the service provider fails to meet the defined service levels, it will be penalized and the customer will receive a credit, or a reduction in the following month's bill. However, if the service provider exceeds the defined performance criteria, it will receive a bonus.

- A service level agreement should have sections addressing privacy and security concerns. It should specify which privacy laws govern, in terms of both context and locale. It should also outline the customer's requirements for data encryption, retention, and deletion.

- An SLA needs to be adaptable. The terms of the agreement should be reviewed periodically and adjusted to reflect changes in market conditions, business requirements, and technology.

Related Resources/Citations

- Health Insurance Portability and Accountability Act, 42 U.S.C. § 1306 (West).
- Fair Credit Reporting Act, 15 U.S.C. §§ 1681-1681(u) (West).
- Gramm-Leach-Bliley Act, 15 U.S.C. §§ 6801-09 (West).
- 35 U.S.C. § 262 (2012).

- *Ethicon, Inc. v. United States Surgical Corp.*, 135 F.3d 1456, 1468 (Fed. Cir. 1998).
- 11 U.S.C. § 365(n) (2012).

Jon Grossman is a partner in the Intellectual Property Practice of Dickstein Shapiro LLP. He practices in the areas of patent law, copyright law, and licensing work with a specialization in issues concerning computer software. He has significant commercial licensing experience encompassing all aspects of contracting, including inbound and outbound licenses, development agreements, Internet contracting, and copyright related agreements. Mr. Grossman also provides clients a full range of IP counseling with a business focus in the areas of strategic acquisitions, outsourcing, and joint ventures and enforcement. Additionally, he works closely with clients in obtaining financing from venture capitalists.

Acknowledgment: *Megan Wood, an associate at Dickstein Shapiro LLP, helped research and write this chapter.*

Megan Wood, an associate at Dickstein Shapiro LLP, focuses on patent litigation and patent prosecution. She graduated magna cum laude from Villanova University School of Law in 2013. During law school, Ms. Wood served as a judicial intern for the Honorable James J. Fitzgerald III, Appellate Judge of the Superior Court of Pennsylvania. Prior to law school, she worked as a mechanical engineer at Lockheed Martin in a research and technology group. She earned a bachelor's of science in chemical and bio-molecular engineering from Johns Hopkins University in 2009. Her concentration was in nanotechnology and interfaces.

Outsourcing Today: Enterprise-Wide Solutions, Smaller Deals, and a Mature Community

Christopher Ford

Partner

Morrison & Foerster LLP

ASPATORE

Introduction

How large the deals are and the nature of what is being outsourced are the most significant changes in outsourcing over the last several years. Except as it relates to purely cloud deals, the methodologies of doing a deal and the structure of those deals have, in large part, reached a level of substantial maturity. Virtually every kind of outsourcing transaction today involves a cloud transaction. Even the large-scale infrastructure deals contain some element of cloud in their solution. Accordingly, companies looking to outsource transactions are faced with many different options of what they can outsource—but those options also create a set of risks and deal dynamics different from traditional outsourcing. These risks for the customer include less control over the outsourced environment, less control over the contracting process and potentially less control over the company's data. Notwithstanding the differences, the cloud model is maturing and these risks will necessarily mitigate as competition increases. This chapter will discuss, in part, how cloud transactions are affecting the sourcing landscape.

For traditional outsourcing transactions, most of the longstanding deal dynamics and practices remain intact. This chapter will discuss some of those dynamics. We will discuss, among other things, the reasons why companies outsource, what should not be outsourced, some of the potential pitfalls and risks in the process, and who the players are.

Current Trends in Sourcing Deals

In outsourcing, the move toward cloud computing is probably the biggest change that we have seen in the last fifteen years. Historically, companies would look for a service provider to provide a solution designed solely for that company. Now, in many disciplines, we see a trend of companies moving away from that traditional model toward a one-size-fits-all solution, often by using cloud computing. Cloud computing, in general terms, is the offering by a service provider of a utility-based service (e.g., applications, infrastructure, or platform). The premise of the model is that the service provider can offer a generic service that the user community can receive without significant modification. Thus, the benefit to the service provider is that it can offer a one-size-fits-nearly-all solution to buyers at a lower price point than if it were providing specified services to those customers. Customers benefit by receiving those services for a lower price if they are willing to forego the flexibility of having a service tailored to them. The move toward cloud computing is changing the way outsourcing deals are transacted as service providers offer utility-based solutions to companies that accept the fact that there are certain kinds of solutions that will not be tailored to their specific needs. Examples of the kinds of solutions we see in today's marketplace include human resources (HR) management applications and functionality, enterprise resource planning systems and e-mail management. For example, service providers specializing in human resources management services can offer an integrated, enterprise-wide solution that can function without a high level of customization. This provides a great economic benefit for any company that is willing to follow the crowd to get what is essentially a bundled price package deal in return for sacrificing their tailored solutions.

Another significant trend relates to the shrinking size and scale of outsourcing transactions. Fifteen years ago, companies going to market sought to outsource entire end-to-end functionality related to its IT infrastructure or a business process to a single provider. In today's world, most companies typically break their outsourcing ventures into smaller component pieces. For example, instead of outsourcing the entire IT infrastructure to one provider, a company may source the data center operations to one provider, break/fix maintenance to another, and help-desk functionality to a third. As a result, instead of having one provider as the integrator, the company becomes the integrator and must manage several different service providers. These smaller deals have led to more competitors in the marketplace, a situation that allows customers to drive down the price because more providers are bidding on the same piece of work. While this may be problematic for the providers who must fight against price pressure and find a balance between offering quality service and maintaining profitability, it is good news for the outsourcing buyers who have more choices at better rates.

The final major trend is that the outsourcing model is maturing. Experienced companies have a better sense of their overall needs, and know what and how to outsource. Companies newer to the outsourcing process often do not have a good sense of the possible outcomes of outsourcing, and do not have a sense of what is beneficial to outsource and what it should keep in house, what their realistic cost savings should be, how to manage service providers in the context of their overall business needs, and a plethora of other issues that companies more mature in the outsourcing model understand. The maturing model, one in which companies have better knowledge and understanding of outsourcing, seems to have created a better overall relationship between customers and providers.

Outsourcing to Achieve Cost Savings, Sustain Company Functions, and Maintain a Competitive Edge

When deciding what (or whether) to outsource, a company must first consider what its goals are in outsourcing, and whether those goals are valid and can be achieved realistically. Companies entering into an outsourcing arrangement often are hoping to achieve some degree of cost savings. Cost savings, as a general principle, is not bad if it is one of several reasons to outsource—but if it is the primary reason, companies can find themselves giving long-term strategic value for short-term gain. Other factors that companies take into account when deciding to outsource include the financial impact of moving a function from a capital expense to an operating expense; the company's ability to sustain a function in-house (i.e., can it financially continue to do what it is currently doing?); whether the company is being disadvantaged in the marketplace compared to its competitors because it has not outsourced these functions (i.e., is it maintaining expenses its competitors have shed?).

Problems in Retaining Necessary Skills

If a company is going to succeed in keeping functions in-house, it must be able to retain or acquire personnel with key skills. In the last few years, the ability to retain and attract talent has come under considerable pressure, particularly as it relates to certain technology skill sets. Part of this issue is an educational gap in the United States with respect to the number of graduating engineers and other technical skilled workers compared to other industrialized countries. The problem is particularly acute in certain geographic regions where local work forces are depleted of certain skill sets. It is not uncommon for companies in certain US regions to outsource (or at least enter into staff augmentation transactions for) portions of their application, development, and maintenance functions because they are not able to obtain the skilled workforce required to do their coding and development. In some respects, this forces many companies to look to the market for help to sustain their core functions.

Outsourcing may also be the only option for a company that must transform its environment. It is not uncommon for companies to refrain from making necessary economic investments in its technologies because it does not have the budget to do so. One example of this has been where companies had developed their critical applications with antiquated code, and then tried to employ new functionality with patches and fixes utilizing that old code. Inevitably, the antiquated code cannot keep up with the requirements of the new functionality. To add to the problem, the people who have the skills to manage the older code begin retiring, leaving the company without the necessary workforce to maintain its systems. This type of problem is especially prevalent in the public sector. To move forward, the company must enter into a transformation that is inevitably costly and disruptive to its environment. Long-term neglect can force a company into a crisis mode where it must do something—either fix it in-house or hire someone to fix and maintain it. Often companies' budgetary cycles do not allow for large capital expenditures to fix these types of problems. Hiring an outsourcer to transform the environment not only allows the company to acquire the necessary skills to accomplish the transformation, but also shifts the capital expense to the service provider. The parties can generally agree upon an economic framework where those costs are absorbed by the company over time, instead of an up-front large-scale investment. These often lead to these costs being accounted for as ongoing operating expenses, as opposed to capital expenses that must be amortized over longer periods.

Outsourcing to Maintain a Competitive Edge

We also see a need for companies to make changes in their environments because they cannot maintain a competitive edge. In today's world where technologies are dictating how quickly a company can get their products to market, companies whose technologies are not keeping pace with their competitors' technologies can find themselves at a competitive disadvantage. A common solution is to hire a service provider that can assist in transforming technologies and business processes, bringing broad industry and best practices to bear. The provider may upgrade and/or run its technology to provide the company with the world-class functionality to allow the business to get to market much more quickly. Companies that engage in this kind of outsourcing are usually more mature in the use of service providers to assist in helping their business objectives. The activities of the service providers in these instances tend to be less in the nature of a commodity provider, and more in the nature of a consultant/business partner. The more successful of these types of arrangements will typically involve some risk and benefit sharing—also known in the industry as gain sharing—and an obligation on the part of the service provider to maintain technologies at industry standards. When engaging in outsourcing projects of these types, cost savings is generally less of a driver (although always a consideration), while business efficiency tends to be more of a focus.

Considerations That May Deter Outsourcing

What Should and Should Not Be Outsourced

Most people believe that the one thing that should not be outsourced is the core functionality of a business. If baking cakes is the core functionality of a business, then the company should not outsource the baker—but it may outsource the janitorial function to maintain optimal cleanliness of the bakery. While this is a crude example, it illustrates an old rule of thumb— that which provides the company its competitive advantage should not be outsourced. Unfortunately, however, we are starting to see a trend of companies outsourcing functions closer to their core functionality, utilizing a layer of management to oversee the new "bakers." The practice may have dangerous long-term impacts, in that it may cause the company to lose some of its skill and knowledge base. This trend demonstrates the changes occurring in today's outsourcing climate. Instead of considering what should *never* be outsourced, companies are more willing to think about what *can* be outsourced on a case-by-case or business-by-business basis.

Impact on Company Culture

The decision of a company to outsource can have long-term impacts on the morale of the workplace. One of the ways companies typically save money in an outsourcing environment is by reducing the headcount. Employees who "survive" through an outsourcing event can often harbor a lack of trust for the institution after the event. There can be a residual feeling that the company does not care about them as individuals, but only cares about improving the bottom line. The employee base can feel less secure about their job, thinking that theirs could be the next job that will be outsourced. This has the potential to create a different (often less desirable) kind of relationship between the company and the workforce. That factor alone may not be enough to keep a company from outsourcing a function, but erosion of culture is an important consideration that must be taken into account. Companies can take a number of steps to mitigate such erosion. For example, a robust honest communication strategy during the outsourcing can help to ease some anxiety. Also, ensuring that some (if not all) of the affected employees will receive job offers from the service provider that are comparable to their current positions helps. For those affected employees not receiving job offers, implementing effective job-reassignment processes are important. Finally, for those affected employees who do not receive job offers from service providers and who cannot be re-assigned within the company, it is key to have out-placement services available, and of course, a healthy severance package, which must be in keeping with general company policies. The ultimate goal is to ensure that the employees who are affected are treated fairly, but those who are left are made to feel that the company continues to care about their jobs.

Loss of Personnel

Another consideration is the potential loss of personnel during the outsourcing process. As soon as the employee base hears that an outsourcing event may occur, many who have a chance of being affected will begin to update their resumes. While it is understood that it is essential for the company to retain certain people who are key to the knowledge base and understand the business, it is also important to make sure that those less critical persons continue to be available to perform the day-to-day activities necessary to maintain operations. Dealing with the former group of employees can be easier than dealing with the latter. The key persons can often be informed that they will land in a good position once the outsourcing is done (either within the company or with the service provider). It is more difficult to make any kind of assurances to the less critical persons, and accordingly, retaining them can be more of a concern. In an effort to retain the necessary staff in the environment to maintain the company's function, companies often provide retention bonuses as a means to entice those persons to stay throughout the outsourcing process. Companies also tie any severance benefits to being employed until completion of the outsourcing process. Because workers are usually concerned about their overall financial security, some are unwilling to hang around for the money, but generally, it will entice enough of the affected employees to stay with the company for operations not to be adversely impacted too severely.

Differences in Promises and Reality

In making the decision to outsource, and in choosing the outsourcer, companies must be able to discern whether the promises that are being made by service providers are fantasy or reality. Outsourcing deals begin with a request for proposals (RFP) process, during which the different service providers offer the company the world—at the lowest possible price and with the highest quality of service. Rarely do those realities align, at least not to the degree promised in RFP responses. More often than not, the promises made and reality achieved in outsourcing deals are far apart. We often see the beginnings of chasm during the transition process—one of the biggest risks points associated with the outsourcing transaction. Generally, the parties agree on a timeline for transition of the services over to the service provider to be completed, with a number of transition projects and milestones to be completed along the way. It is not uncommon for these timelines to fall apart. Most often, the owners of the outsourcing deal within the company have made promises to their executives and business stakeholders about when something will be done and the resources that will be required to make that happen. When the service provider cannot deliver in that timeframe, the owners of the deal are left to explain the disruption to their organization. This creates stress on the entire relationship at the very beginning of the relationship—during the honeymoon phase. It is often the first point of contention seen in a deal and sometimes it can ruin entire transactions.

Accordingly, companies and service providers must conduct adequate due diligence during the outsourcing process and stress test the solutions being proposed. Even well-intentioned plans can go awry if necessary information is not shared, proper planning has not been conducted, and adequate time has not been built into the timeline for unexpected occurrences.

The Potential for Failure to Achieve Cost Savings

Another risk for companies is the failure to achieve the desired cost savings from the outsourcing arrangement. In every deal, the customer does an economic analysis examining its current spend on the function and what the service providers claim they will be able to save by outsourcing that function. It is not uncommon for the deal owner in the company (e.g., the chief information officer in an IT deal) to make promises to the chief financial officer that the transaction will save significant money over the term of the agreement, most of which will occur in the first few years of the term. The CFO, taking the word of the executive, counts on those savings in its earnings projections. If (and most likely when) those cost savings are not fully realized, the CFO will come back to the executive looking for answers. If for no other reason than personal survival within the organization, it is important for deal owners to be cautious in their estimates of cost savings in outsourcing transactions. History has shown that it is rare that an outsourcing deal will achieve the anticipated overall cost savings, especially during the first fiscal year, because problems always arise that drive costs higher than expected.

For these reasons, it is important to advise clients to set realistic expectations regarding what providers can and will offer before entering into an outsourcing deal. The client must consider the realistic timelines and risks, and evaluate the promises that the service providers make to the business community in terms of operational effectiveness and financial savings and whether those promises realistically can be met through outsourcing. Thankfully, some of the problem has been mitigated in recent years by the fact that the models are maturing, and as more companies gain extensive outsourcing experience, they begin to realistically evaluate the capabilities of their potential service providers and their solutions.

Successfully Choosing an Appropriate Outsourcing Provider

Most companies choosing outsourcing providers look for the following four essential components, in no particular order: First, they want to choose a provider that will help them achieve their financial goals (i.e., costs savings). Second, if transformation is a key to the arrangement, they look for a provider that will be able to create the desired operational and business change in the environment. Third, they want a provider that will be able to either maintain or improve the company's quality of service while giving them access to industry best practices, new technologies and skilled workers. Finally, they consider the "fit," choosing a provider with whom their organization will be able to work well.

It is not uncommon for companies to discount in many cases, or in some cases to completely overlook, the fit issue. Particularly companies that are less mature in the outsourcing model may be unaware that some of the service providers are rigid in the way they deliver their services, and that regardless of what the contract says, that service provider will perform the function in the manner it typically does. Service providers do this because it is the most cost efficient way for them to deliver the services, but such rigidity may not work well with the culture and business processes of the outsourcing customer. Even when it is likely that the outsourcing company can benefit from some of that rigidity to assist it in operating more efficiently and in a disciplined manner, the customer's organization may not be able to operationally or culturally absorb that kind of change. Experience shows that those kinds of organizations do not tend to work well together.

Ensuring That the Service Level Agreement Is Favorable to the Company

Agreement on service level agreements (SLAs) in an outsourcing deal often creates tension between the customer and the service provider. Customers believe that they are buying world-class processes, technologies, skill, and know-how from the service providers and therefore the service providers should be able to perform functions with a higher degree of quality than the customer was able to perform for itself. Service providers, on the other hand, do not want to commit to performing at a higher level than the customer previously performed. We advise our clients that if their environments were not operating at world-class levels prior to the outsourcing they should not expect the service provider to operate at those levels afterward. However, we also advise them against accepting the company's prior performance as the standard. The service provider does bring expertise to the relationship and the customer should expect that the service provider can perform better; but the service provider must operate within certain constraints, including, but not limited to, the customer's operating environment, quality of the customer's technology with which the service provider must interface, the solution that the customer chooses, resource availability of the customer to cooperate with the service provider in performing the services, and so on. The companies must be willing and able to reach fair compromises on service levels that give the customer the benefit of hiring an expert, but not burdening the service provider with unrealistic expectations.

The advisors to the customer, attorneys, and consultants, must assist the customer in determining the metrics that the business needs to operate. The company must understand its business needs and translate those into how efficiently the service provider can offer those service levels. Attorneys and consultants typically advise the company not to attempt to force service providers into service levels that will require the service provider to create unnecessary redundancy. Redundancy will always cost, and if the higher service level does not satisfy a bona fide business requirement, the cost associated with such redundancy may be an unnecessary expenditure (potentially eroding some of the promised cost savings). While it might sound good to have five "9s" as a service level, if there is no operational difference to having four "9s," and the lower service level will allow for a less costly solution because less redundancy is required, the better business result would be to require four "9s."

Another pitfall to the SLA process is that both the company and the service provider often lose sight of the fact that the actual purpose of the service levels is to modify behavior and not penalize service providers for inadequate performance. With this in mind, the attorney should attempt to contractually create a structure whereby the service provider is forced to perform the services in a way that is most beneficial to the customer. The contract should require the service provider to dedicate or allocate resources to service areas that are most important to the company, which means the company must prioritize services, understanding in which area it is willing to sacrifice service delivery for an area where it wants to emphasize improved performance. It is easy for providers and customers to get lost in the concept of a service level credit for a failed service level being a type of a remedy. The provider may attempt to declare the service level credit a sole and exclusive remedy, but credits can never be remedies for performance failures; the credits are almost always too small to make the customer whole for the service delivery failure. Instead, focusing on the premise that service levels are intended to be an economic means of modifying behavior, the parties can design a structure that forces resource allocation to the services that meets the needs of the customer.

Creating the appropriate risk profile is the beginning of the SLA structuring issues—that is, ensuring that enough of the service provider's profits are at stake for them to take appropriate measures to avoid losing that money. In addition, the service levels must be weighted in such a way that allows the customer to emphasize which ones are more important to it; thus, when one is failed, the economic impact to the service provider is greater. This will give the service provider incentive to put more resources on those service levels that are weighted more heavily. Finally the customer must be able to modify the weighting relatively frequently if it needs to change its business priorities, or if it needs to cause the service providers to emphasize a service delivery area where performance has been weaker. There are a number of tried-and-true structures that outsourcing lawyers have used to achieve these results.

Engaging the Necessary Players to Ensure Outsourcing Arrangement Success

The participation of several key players is usually necessary to make an outsourcing arrangement successful. The process starts with an executive from the customer who has the vision to outsource a function as a key driver to the business; someone with a wide viewpoint who can consider how the deal will affect not only that particular function, but also the company as a whole. He or she must then gain the support of the business owners who are affected by the function, as they are the ones who ultimately must accept the fact that someone outside of the company will be performing the work. Obviously, business owner support is essential, as outsourcing arrangements are usually disruptive, particularly during the transition phase. In addition, business owners also can be asked to dedicate additional resources to the function being outsourced to deal with the change. Few outsourcing deals are successful without strong support from the business stakeholders.

The company's financial community should also be involved from the start. Since cost savings usually drive the deal, someone from the chief financial officer's team should monitor the entire process. In addition, management of the function must be intimately involved because they know how it works, what the business pitfalls are, and what it will take to successfully transition the function to a third party. Sometimes gaining support of the management can become a struggle, since people closest to the function are also likely to be the ones negatively affected by the venture. Failure to successfully onboard the key manager in the process can create a barrier to any deal getting done since that person is usually the one with most of the key operational information. If the company intends to transition some of its personnel to the service provider or to reduce its workforce because of the outsourcing, human resources must be involved to manage the process. Of course, depending on the deal, many other customer personnel may be necessary to make it successful, including but not limited to internal communications, tax professionals, audit professionals, and the technical subject matter experts.

In today's more mature outsourcing world, many companies employ people to manage the entire process. These people typically include the aforementioned employees within the company, as well as an external consulting advisor. The consultant usually assists in the business aspects of assembling the deal, including drafting the RFP's necessary components (such as the services that will be delivered, pricing, service levels, and account governance). The company should also include lawyers early in the process so they are better able to structure the deal appropriately to achieve the best outcome for the client.

Conclusion

Currently, we are not seeing a huge amount of change in the outsourcing environment; instead, there have been continued modifications, such as the continued movement into the cloud environment. This is likely to continue as it has during the last few years, although cloud providers are beginning to acquiesce more to the needs of their particular client bases. In the past, cloud providers provided non-negotiable contracts and forced their customers to move forward with those terms, but with more competition in the cloud marketplace, customers are now able to push back on some key issues that are most important to them, typically those that involve data privacy and security. Cloud service providers are also beginning to offer some audit rights in response to changes in the regulatory environment. For example, regulators in the financial services industry require several components to outsourcing deals, so in an effort to market their product in the financial services space, cloud service providers have recognized the necessity of making changes in the way they do business. These small factors are shifting the needle in customers' favor within the cloud environment, but simply finding middle ground is bound to be a slow process.

In a maturing market, the need for more experienced outsourcing lawyers is heightened. It is important that companies hire lawyers who have extensive knowledge of how relationships work in any transaction, whether it is a cloud transaction, regular outsourcing, or any kind of services arrangement. They must understand how the two parties will react to different stimuli and structure their client's deals appropriately. We continue to believe that we are a valuable part of the process, but that we must provide more to the transaction than just knowing how to do a deal—we must be the conduits that help our clients understand the shifting marketplace and how their businesses fit into the framework. It is our job to help the clients achieve efficient, effective transactions that will result in positive customer/provider relationships over the term of the agreement.

Key Takeaways

- Ensure the impact of outsourcing a particular function is always on your client's mind. Outsourcing can change the relationship between the company and its workforce, and result in the loss of personnel, the failure of the provider to live up to promises, and the business's failure to achieve cost savings.
- Advise your clients to set realistic expectations regarding what providers can and will offer before entering into an outsourcing

deal. The client must consider the realistic timelines and risks, and evaluate the promises that the executives make to the business community in terms of operational effectiveness and financial savings, and whether those promises realistically can be met through outsourcing.

- Encourage your client choosing an outsourcing provider to look for four essential components: the provider should help them achieve financial success; the provider should be able to create the operational change in the environment necessary for them to achieve their operational and business goals; the provider should be able to either maintain or improve the company's quality of service; and the provider must be an organization with whom they will be able to work well.

- Make sure your client has involved the correct people in the outsourcing venture. In addition to the business owners, HR and personnel with knowledge about the function being outsourced can help facilitate an easier transition. A chief financial officer should oversee the financial aspects of the deal. An external consulting advisor can also assist in the RFP process.

Christopher Ford is a partner with Morrison & Foerster LLP, and is the chair of the firm's Global Sourcing Group. His practice focuses on advising customers on the full life cycle of their complex information technology and business process outsourcing transactions. He also advises clients on joint ventures and telecommunications and licensing transactions, as well as enterprise resource planning and other systems integration.

Mr. Ford works closely with some of the leading global outsourcing consultancies and has a deep understanding of the sourcing process and how to use it to best represent his clients. In addition to advising on legal issues in a sourcing transaction, Mr. Ford counsels his clients on business issues such as the best use of available outsourcing models and how to engage effectively with service providers to ensure delivery of robust and long-term service solutions.

A Perfect Storm: Risk Management Tools for the Confluence of Increased Regulatory Oversight, Cloud Services, and BOYD

Peter R. George

Partner

Baker & McKenzie LLP

ASPATORE

Introduction: Outsourcing Issues and Trends

Important outsourcing trends that clients need to be aware of include the increased focus on risk management, particularly with respect to the management of regulatory and legal compliance risk, data protection, and security risk, and risks associated with downstream third- and fourth-party providers. These risks are further amplified by the loss of control some clients find over the procurement of low- or no-cost cloud-based solutions and the increasingly global nature of most solutions. For many clients, a key emerging challenge to managing outsourcing risk is identifying the outsourcing transactions in the first place (which are increasingly hidden under the term cloud or are procured by employees for use on bring your own devices or BYOD) and implementing appropriate controls to ensure that those transactions are managed robustly and in compliance with the client's risk management policies and procedures, especially where low up-front investment costs or no initial capital expenditure may not trigger existing oversight policies.

Factors behind Emerging Trends

These risks are emerging through the confluence of three important factors.

Regulatory Interest in Use of Third-Party Providers

First, as enterprises increasingly rely on third-party providers to perform critical functions and share important information regarding their customers with those third-party providers, regulators are taking notice. This interest is further heightened by the lingering impact of the financial crisis, which many consider was caused by under-appreciated systemic risks and lack of effective controls over risk management. Regulators are showing increasing concern over examining the scope of activities being outsourced to third parties, the diligence that outsourcing customers exercise in entering into such relationships, and the practices that customers use to measure and manage those relationships.

For example, globally, there is an increased regulatory concern over the management of risk related to third-party service agreements—including outsourcing agreements—in the financial services and insurance verticals.

The recent release of OCC Bulletin 2013-29 on Risk Management Guidance for Third-Party Relationships in the United States focuses on risk management across the entire lifecycle of outsourcing transactions in the banking vertical. The bulletin emphasizes the importance of board-level oversight of these transactions. Similarly, in Hong Kong, the Office of the Commissioner of Insurance recently promulgated a Guidance Note on Outsourcing (GN 14). GN 14 requires notice to the insurance regulator of material outsourcings, which notices must disclose to the regulator the processes and tools used to manage the risks inherent to engaging a third party to perform critical business functions. For example, if a contract is used as a tool for managing sourcing risk, the contract should be disclosed to the regulatory body. These are just two examples of the increased attention that regulators are showing toward outsourcing transactions around the world.

We expect that as regulators continue to look at the risks involved in today's complex, extended enterprises, with critical activities being provided by third parties all around the world, regulatory interest in and oversight of outsourcing transactions will only increase. In addition, the ease with which data flows around the world will continue to strain internal compliance offices and regulators working to satisfy the legal protections afforded to personal data across the globe. In part, the complexity of managing data flows will likely increasingly be addressed through technology. However, there also will be a significant and growing demand for guidance in balancing the risks and demands of legal and compliance burdens in the data protection and privacy space against the necessity of cross-border data transfers. There will also be more large and notorious data breach events and a demand for solutions to counter the ever-present and growing risk of cybercrime. One way to address these risks, we expect, will be to work with service providers that are experts in the area and can leverage the costs of investing in addressing these issues across a wide customer base.

Cloud Solutions Requiring Little or No Capital Investment

Second, as cloud technologies allow suppliers broad opportunities to leverage infrastructure across clients, solutions that in the past may have required a significant up-front capital investment can now be provided in a service model with much lower or no capital investment. This technological advance has brought forth a tidal wave of cloud solutions, many of which require little or no up-front capital investment to implement and do not require long-term contractual commitments. As a result, clients may find it more difficult to apply risk management processes that are triggered by capital expenditures or budget thresholds as a means of controlling the risks related to implementing these solutions.

In the past, many businesses would manage information technology risks through budget management processes that would require board approval prior to any significant capital investment or any commitment for long-term operational expenditures. This worked where outsourcing transactions required large capital investments or extended contractual commitments. In the context of cloud solutions, where a supplier's hardware investments are leveraged across a customer base and designed to support multi-tenancy, there is often less need for large up-front capital investments to adopt a solution and there is often no requirement to make long-term financial commitments. As a result, activities that may have previously required board oversight, such as information technology infrastructure deployment and management, may not trigger the risk management controls that would have previously guaranteed a minimum level of diligence and oversight over these types of transactions. Instead of calling it outsourcing, it is marketed as cloud.

However, the impact of the service to the business may rise to the same level as an outsourcing and present many of the same risks. The importance of information technology infrastructure management and the enterprise's dependence on that infrastructure (and the data flowing through it) does not change even if it is called cloud instead of "managed services," and the transaction still merits a high level of review. To address this fact, we are seeing many businesses changing their oversight control requirements and focusing less on budget authority and more on the business risk of the transaction, with cloud transactions often triggering higher levels of oversight than procurement transactions of equal or even lower budgets.

In addition, because these solutions often leverage supplier or third-party technology investments, critical business and customer information is often held outside of the enterprise's own information systems. This gives rise to the potential for such cloud services to comprise critical aspects of a client's business, including customer relationship management, human resources, and billing and to put at risk the trust that consumers, suppliers and business partners place on their relationship with such enterprises. In many cases, regulators will likely classify such transactions as outsourcings, even if that term is not used to describe the cloud services transaction.

Unfortunately, it is becoming routine to hear about data security breaches involving the disclosure of personal information, including customer credit card information, where that data is held or processed for an enterprise by third-party service providers, or even where a supplier merely has access to an enterprise's network. Even in that context, though, it is often the enterprise's name and reputation—and not the name of the third-party service provider—that makes news. As a result, enterprises are rethinking existing environmental and security control requirements to ensure that the risks of using third parties to collect, maintain, and store information are properly assessed even where no up-front capital expenditures are required to implement third-party solutions. In other words, the controls that exist to manage and govern outsourcing transactions are being applied to the cloud.

I expect that this focus on information security risk management will continue to grow. In addition, though, I also expect a continued increase in the global reach of cybercrime, with data security breaches being perpetrated by criminals around the world. In the context of outsourcing solutions, we think this will cause enterprises to further scrutinize their third-party solutions and the architecture of those solutions, the delivery locations where the infrastructure of those solutions reside, and the relationships that service providers have with their subcontractors. We are already seeing suppliers developing solutions that provide customers with information about and even direct contractual privity to fourth-tier providers. We expect that this trend will continue and that customers and suppliers will continue to work together to identify and address the risks inherent to global service solutions.

One way we are seeking to address these issues is through the development of tools to help clients analyze the risk of engaging cloud services providers and products to help those clients address the risks raised through due diligence, contract terms, monitoring and reporting, and ongoing vendor management. Useful tools include template cloud services agreements that are useful in ensuring that key risks are identified and addressed when contracting for such services. Alternatively, cloud services procurement policies and procedures, including handbooks with checklists and approved sample provisions, are useful in vetting supplier template agreements. We are also working with buyers and suppliers to help focus attention on these issues, evaluate market trends and solutions to these issues, and share information.

Employee Use of Personal Devices for Work

Third, as technology becomes more ubiquitous, employees increasingly use their own devices, such as smartphones and tablets, for work-related activities. Many enterprises manage risks related to technology through their information technology offices and their controls on the procurement of information technology assets. Where employees increasingly make procurement decisions about technologies used to do the business of the enterprise, the information technology office and the robust information technology procurement controls used to mitigate risks related to technology procurement become less helpful in managing and mitigating technology risks. Instead, enterprises must look beyond those controls to identify and implement risk management controls sufficient to address a global workplace where individual employees will increasingly make their own decisions about workplace tools.

For example, many of our clients have found employees increasingly making use of privately procured equipment and applications to perform their jobs. BYOD is becoming commonplace. But even as enterprises start addressing their policies on physical assets, employees are moving beyond the physical asset and adopting personal digital services as well. For example, employees may place critical business information in "Dropbox" or store customer contact information in a personal application. In many cases, business tools that employees previously would have had to rely on their employer to provide are now available free of charge on the Internet. This technology is often critical to the employees' ability to do their jobs. Why not take advantage of it?

In some cases, enterprises have policies or procedures in place restricting the use of personal devices and applications. However, these policies and procedures are often not well enforced. In other cases, those policies and procedures are simply not written yet or are written to reflect a time when technology was provided and owned by the employer. In fact, in many cases, these policies rely on the employer's ownership of the technology as the justification for controlling the use of the technology and the business information flowing through it. In most cases, companies do not realize that they are outsourcing technology procurement to their employees or that such practices raise the same risks and issues as outsourcing that activity to a third party.

Moreover, even while employers are getting their arms around managing the risk of outsourcing technology procurement to their employees, those employees are increasingly finding low-cost opportunities to outsource tasks and activities to other third parties. For example, employees may use their own instant messaging service to communicate about work-related activities. Companies that would never have considered adopting communications technologies hosted by third parties with whom they have no contract find themselves beholden to service providers selected by their employees. Couple this with the increasing focus on legal and regulatory compliance discussed earlier, and the result is a fairly complicated challenge for large enterprises: to manage the risk associated with cloud technologies and personally owned devices against the loss of the enterprise's control over such technologies in the face of greater scrutiny over legal and regulatory compliance. What, in other words, are compliance officers supposed to do?

To manage such risks, we are seeing enterprises more actively manage BYOD initiatives and employee use of personally owned applications through policies, information controls, approved resource portals, training, and ongoing evaluation. For example, many clients are reviewing and updating antiquated information technology usage policies. Many of these policies focus on asset ownership as justification for access and control over information. These policies are being revised to focus less on the ownership of IT assets and instead more on the business purpose for which an asset is used. Likewise, more attention is being focused on the nature of the information that employees may produce, collect, and store than on the ownership of the assets used to produce, collect, and store that information. We expect that this interest in and review of policies will continue. In many respects, this is similar to the attention paid in outsourcing agreements to data ownership, protection, and control. These policies will likely continue to evolve and we expect many enterprises will likely adopt the tools used to manage risk in outsourcing transactions to protect enterprise business information in the BYOD context.

Many enterprises are restructuring the technical architecture of their businesses to focus on enterprise networks as the repository for employee, customer, and other business information and assets. For example, many enterprises have policies restricting employees from storing business information on personal devices and instead require that personal devices interface with firm assets only through connections to enterprise networks. In many ways, this is similar to the technical architecture of software application and development outsourcing transactions, where third-party programmers access the enterprise's network remotely to perform their business activities, with no data being stored in the service provider's environment or on service provider equipment.

Likewise, employees may be restricted from using third-party applications to perform business services, unless those applications are procured by the employee from an enterprise-managed repository or portal. This architecture permits the enterprise to perform diligence and monitor the applications and third-party service providers that their employees are using, establish enterprise-wide contracts with such third-party service providers, and track the usage of those applications. It also allows the enterprise to ensure that it has access to and control over the information technology systems that the employee is using and access to the business data that the employee creates. Essentially, the employee has flexibility to use the tools he or she deems necessary, but only after the employer has diligently addressed the risks of using such technology and taken appropriate steps to mitigate and manage such risks.

Managing the complexity of such environments, where multiple employee-owned devices are connected to enterprise networks, will continue to evolve. The good news is that there are tools available to aid enterprises in managing this complexity. We expect that those tools will reflect many of the risk mitigation practices that have evolved in the outsourcing space. However, it is important that clients are proactive in this area. What the enterprise does not know—especially in a world where data breach is becoming more common and where cyber criminals lurk cleverly online—can hurt it. No enterprise, especially heavily regulated enterprises with access to and responsibility for critical client information, would entrust that information to a third party without doing appropriate diligence and taking appropriate steps to protect that information. Its employees should not either. We expect that enterprises will continue to focus attention on this area going forward.

The confluence of increased regulatory oversight and interest in sourcing transactions—combined with low-cost cloud services and increased employee access to and control over business technologies—is creating a "perfect storm" for global enterprises. Just as those entities are being forced to cede control over business technologies to their employees, regulators are stepping up their interest in third-party solutions. Many enterprises will be reluctant to address the issues that this perfect storm raises and will hide from the fact that employees are using third-party technologies to get the job done. Others will embrace this challenge and develop policies and solutions to steer a clear course through this unprecedented period of change. In any case, I think these trends will continue and that, ultimately, those entities that embrace these trends boldly will maximize the value and minimize the risks associated with them.

Regionalization and Globalization of Service Delivery

A related emerging trend is the regionalization and globalization of service delivery made possible through communications technologies. Business support services that previously would have been required to be provided locally by a global enterprise's local entity in each country where that entity has offices (such as technology infrastructure support, application development and maintenance, finance and accounting, procurement, customer relationship management, even engineering support services), can now be provided remotely from anywhere in the world to anywhere in the world. This creates tremendous opportunities for innovation, cost reduction, and even risk management. On the other hand, it also exposes the global enterprise to risks that previously did not exist, including political risk, compliance risk, and environmental risks.

Moreover, even where captive entities are used to manage such risks, from a regulatory perspective, most jurisdictions treat shared services centers as third-party relationships. Therefore, particularly for clients in highly regulated industries like financial services, insurance, and pharmaceuticals, managing regulatory compliance risk requires significant up-front planning. These clients must also invest in service relationship lifecycle management, including due diligence, contracting, and supplier management. We are increasingly seeing enterprises in other less-regulated industries make investments in supplier lifecycle management to identify, mitigate, and manage third-party relationship risks.

As a result of these trends, we are seeing enterprises look at outsourcing not simply as a means of reducing costs, but increasingly as a way to take advantage of best practices to mitigate regulatory and compliance risks. The use of regional centers of excellence is one example of how sourcing can be used as a risk reduction tool. For clients with business processes being performed locally, sourcing that service from a regional center of excellence allows the enterprise to exercise greater control over the processes used to deliver the service. This regionalization of service delivery can help ensure that controls are compliant with regulatory requirements and appropriately documented. It can also facilitate better review and oversight of the implementation of such controls. For example, with respect to information security controls, the regionalization of company data centers can help an enterprise ensure that appropriate security controls are in place, if for no other reason than such controls may be monitored across a more limited number of environments.

Clearly, however, not all business functions can be migrated to regional delivery centers. In regulated industries like insurance, functions that may be performed only by licensed professionals may have to be performed locally. For example, some jurisdictions require that soliciting the purchase or sale of insurance products be performed by licensed brokers. Migrating such activities to offshore suppliers may not comply with local regulatory requirements. In addition, enterprises may have local expertise and know how that provides the enterprise with a competitive advantage. Such expertise should not be outsourced to third parties and may not even be migrated to a captive delivery center.

Where, however, support services are outsourced, enterprises must manage the risks associated with outsourcing such services to third parties. In some industry verticals, this may be required. For example, OCC Bulletin 2013-29 (described earlier) sets out the third-party lifecycle risk management processes that US banks should follow when outsourcing services. Likewise, GN 14 provides risk management requirements for insurance companies that outsource material activities in Hong Kong. However, even in industries or jurisdictions where third-party relationships are less heavily regulated, enterprises are increasingly leveraging sourcing risk management strategies to identify and mitigate the risks of outsourcing.

These risk management practices tend to be based on the lifecycle of third-party sourcing arrangements commencing with planning around the third-party service engagement, through qualifying suppliers through due diligence; contract structuring and negotiation; and ultimately through engagement, management, and termination of the third-party relationship. One increasingly common attribute of such risk management practices is a focus on leveraging the supplier's skills and experience providing services to multiple customers with the enterprise's in-depth experience regarding its business and customers. In many ways, while the enterprise ultimately retains responsibility for its regulatory compliance obligations, suppliers that are able to support the enterprise's compliance efforts are able to offer and demonstrate significant advantages to their customers.

Often, the success and cost of satisfying compliance burdens rests on cooperation between the enterprise and supplier. For example, in many cases, regulatory compliance will require contractual privity between customers and suppliers of outsourced services. Where this contractual privity involves multiple customer entities all sourcing the same services from the same supplier entity or entities (and its and their tiers of subcontractors), suppliers that have evolved procedures or authorization practices to facilitate the execution of all those contracts can provide their customers with significantly more value than those that either do not recognize the need for local privity or that have not undertaken the internal work necessary to make such contractual privity possible. Likewise, customers that have figured out how to structure their relationships to meet these regulatory burdens find that those structures are leverageable across their base of shared services investments.

The use of sourcing as a tool to manage risk is somewhat different from earlier drivers of outsourcing, which often focused more on cost savings, operational excellence, and technical innovation. While these three legs of the outsourcing stool continue to be key value drivers for outsourcing, risk mitigation is emerging as a fourth pillar supporting the outsourcing business case. This is particularly true in areas where suppliers are investing in and developing risk management expertise, such as information security, records management, and other similar areas. We expect that these solutions will become increasingly more attractive to enterprise customers as risk management and mitigation continues to evolve. For counsel advising clients on these issues, I would expect that there would be considerable opportunities to work with sourcing advisors to build out this fourth pillar.

Conclusion

The explosion of cloud services and BYOD initiatives—coupled with increased regulation and regulatory interest in outsourcing—is creating a perfect storm for global enterprises. Some enterprises will hide from this storm, while others will embrace it and use sourcing as a tool to manage these risks. By standardizing processes and managing these risks end to end, global enterprises will be able to position themselves to take advantage of the opportunities that these trends make available. We expect that those enterprises will be the most successful.

Key Takeaways

- Risk management practices that focus on capital expenditure approvals or approvals for long-term contractual commitments may not be appropriate for cloud solutions. Instead, risk management should focus on the sensitivity of the data being processed and the criticality of the service to the enterprise.
- Cloud transactions raise data security and control risks similar to traditional outsourcing transactions and the tools used to manage those risks should be considered when assessing cloud solutions.
- To mitigate threats posed by BYOD, policies can be revised to focus less on the ownership of IT assets and instead more on the business purpose for which an asset is used.

- Policies restricting employees from storing business information on personal devices, and instead requiring that personal devices interface with firm assets only through connections to enterprise networks can help protect information.

- Enterprises may look to outsourcing not simply as a means of reducing costs, but increasingly as a way to take advantage of best practices to mitigate regulatory and compliance risks. The use of regional centers of excellence is one example of how sourcing can be used as a risk reduction tool.

Peter R. George, a partner with Baker & McKenzie LLP, advises information technology companies on various aspects of their domestic and foreign operations. He has prepared numerous short articles on marketing and protecting software, computer and telecommunication products and services, as well as outsourcing. Early in his practice, Mr. George acted as associate counsel for small and medium-sized companies, helping them acquire an in-depth understanding of their core products, as well as the legal issues related to their delivery over the Internet and through traditional means.

Climate Change: Cloud Sourcing as the New Normal for IT Outsourcing Transactions

Emma Maconick

Partner

King & Spalding

ASPATORE

Introduction

Cloud sourcing[1] is to its traditional outsourcing[2] counterpart what climate change is to our daily environment—it pushes existing weather patterns to their logical extremes. It is the disruptive force that will require customers and providers of outsourced technologies—and the legal professionals who serve them—to recalibrate their sourcing methodology and agreements to the new normal. Just as extreme weather incidents are becoming part of our meteorological lexicon, cloud sourcing is part of the new standard operating procedure (SOP) for how businesses are approaching outsourcing. While there are many similarities between traditional IT outsourcing and cloud sourcing, the contracts for the provision or receipt of those services must be approached by legal practitioners in some fundamentally different ways.

This chapter will provide a primer on the technological advances that made cloud sourcing ubiquitous, explore how the allocation of risk that typically plays out between customer and vendor of traditional outsourcing services no longer makes sense when applied to a cloud sourcing agreement and provide some practical guidance on how to solve that challenge in the agreement, and discuss what traditional IT outsourcing maxims remain true as applied to the cloud sourcing model.

We Are Not in Kansas Anymore…

To appreciate the impact of the cloud[3] on how business does business, we need to understand the technological backdrop that enabled what will likely be seen as the first step toward the fourth IT Industrial Revolution.[4] The advent of machine virtualization[5] has led to the disaggregation of the

---

[1] U.S. Dep't of Commerce, National Institute of Standards and Technology, *Cloud Computing Synopsis and Recommendations*, (May 2012), *available at* http://csrc.nist.gov/publications/nistpubs/800-146/sp800-146.pdf

[2] *Id.*

[3] *Id.*

[4] After mainframes, personal computers, and the Internet, the fourth IT Industrial Revolution is the "Internet of Things:" a "network of physical objects that contain embedded technology to communicate and sense or interact with their internal states or the external environment" wirelessly or via an Internet cloud-based system. *See* Gartner, IT Glossary, *Internet of Things*, *available at* http://www.gartner.com/it-glossary/internet-of-things/.

[5] Virtualization means to create a virtual version of a device or resource, such as a server, storage device, network, or even an operating system where the framework divides the

traditional technology stack[6] that was historically handed over wholesale to traditional IT services providers. The traditional technical architectures tended to require data and systems to be tightly integrated, and as a consequence, they were inflexible and expensive to change. Virtualization has allowed new computing architectures that can be loosely and flexibly interlinked and managed. As a result, virtually any functionality or process that an organization might need can be partitioned out and provided or sourced "as a service" through parallel, non-coterminous agreements to the point where infrastructure as a service (IaaS)[7], platform as a service (PaaS),[8] and software as a service (SaaS)[9] are now the standard service models for cloud sourcing.

What used to be the infrastructure layer—a network of servers equipped with load balancers, firewalls, and virtual private networks (VPNs) that handled data processing and storage—is now provided as IaaS, where the

---

resource into one or more execution environments. Even something as simple as partitioning a hard drive is considered virtualization because you take one drive and partition it to create two separate hard drives. Devices, applications, and human users are able to interact with the virtual resource as if it were a real single logical resource. Webopedia, *virtualization, available at* http://www.webopedia.com/TERM/V/virtualization.html.

[6] At its simplest, the "stack" refers to the infrastructure layer that underpins the platform layer on which the application layer runs.

[7] *Infrastructure as a Service* (IaaS). The capability provided to the consumer is to provision processing, storage, networks, and other fundamental computing resources where the consumer is able to deploy and run arbitrary software, which can include operating systems and applications. The consumer does not manage or control the underlying cloud infrastructure but has control over operating systems, storage, and deployed applications; and possibly limited control of select networking components (e.g., host firewalls). *See* U.S. Dep't of Commerce, National Institute of Standards and Technology, *The NIST Definition of Cloud Computing*, (Sept. 2011), *available at* http://csrc.nist.gov/publications/nistpubs/800-145/SP800-145.pdf.

[8] *Platform as a Service* (PaaS). The capability provided to the consumer is to deploy onto the cloud infrastructure consumer-created or acquired applications created using programming languages, libraries, services, and tools supported by the provider. The consumer does not manage or control the underlying cloud infrastructure including network, servers, operating systems, or storage, but has control over the deployed applications and possibly configuration settings for the application-hosting environment. *Id.* at 2.

[9] *Software as a Service* (SaaS). The capability provided to the consumer is to use the provider's applications running on a cloud infrastructure. The applications are accessible from various client devices through either a thin client interface, such as a web browser (e.g., web-based email), or a program interface. The consumer does not manage or control the underlying cloud infrastructure including network, servers, operating systems, storage, or even individual application capabilities, with the possible exception of limited user-specific application configuration settings. *Id.* at 2.

service component is the provision of infrastructure management software that allows a consumer to easily obtain new computing resources. The value driver in IaaS is that it allows organizations to rent infrastructure instead of purchasing it, thereby significantly reducing their capital expenditure (and carbon footprint) in one fell swoop and having that infrastructure managed by a provider who should, by definition, be better equipped to do so than the customer. What used to be the platform layer—operating systems and integrated infrastructure that provided an environment for conducting common development tasks—is now known as PaaS. The service component is using the providers' architecture and tools that solve common software development problems such as how to collect, store, retrieve, search, and analyze data during the software development process, rather than spending time and resources resolving those endemic problems each time. What used to be the application layer—software programs consisting of executable files—is now being provided as SaaS, where the service provider allows the customer to use its cloud-based applications on-demand. The value add of SaaS is that the customer can structure a deal whereby it just pays for the service it needs rather than having to contract for peak capacity and leaving applications largely sitting idle; and the chosen application is likely to be a more elegant solution than what any customer could build in-house in the time and with the resources it has to address the problem.

The Cloud as a Variant, More Evolved Form of Outsourcing

This evolution toward cloud-based service delivery systems means that customers are getting on-demand, scalable solutions they need from a marketplace of thousands, rather than tens, of increasingly trusted providers, allowing them to be flexible with respect to operating expenditure and make little or no capital expenditure. In addition, cloud sourcing is a more environmentally conscious choice that allows organizations to start small, then scale up quickly if a given solution works, theoretically getting automatic service integration and software upgrades easily, with less change management.

Cloud sourcing is far less mature than outsourcing, but has far-reaching implications for customers and providers because it involves the automation of a process rather than the simple transfer of the process (often unchanged) to an outsourcer. While there are important differences between the cloud-based service models and traditional outsourcing, they should be seen as part of the same continuum, rather than opposing ends in a binary decision tree. This is especially so, as the traditional outsourcing providers are embracing and deploying cloud technologies themselves as part of their own outsourcing offerings. The more customers shift from using the cloud as a short-term, tactical option to a more long-term, transformational, and strategic solution, the IT infrastructure of the future will likely consist of a mixture of in-house software and systems, automated functions, cloud services, and some outsourced operations—all interwoven with various degrees of complexity.

Companies will continue to outsource, but the decisions on what to outsource and where and how are nowhere near as easy as practitioners once thought with the advent and rapid prevalence of cloud-based solutions. Any organization consists of a string of resources such as storage, data, systems, network, and so on and the cloud sits alongside them, but it represents a new way of approaching an old problem.

Legal Challenges

Now that anyone within an organization can source a cloud solution on provider-friendly, B2C-oriented terms with the swipe of a corporate credit card, companies are increasingly having to invest in cloud sourcing policies and leaning on their legal advisors to help put them together. These policies require the procurer to develop a business case, conduct some basic diligence, undergo a legal risk analysis, and develop a sign-off process.

The legal analysis should include asking:

- What is the financial stability of the provider?
- What are the limits on liability imposed in the contract?
- What kind of audit rights do I need to have?
- How does this provider solve the regulatory and compliance requirements of my business?
- How does this provider handle e-discovery?
- Where are this provider's data centers?

- What level of data security are they providing and how safe is my data?
- What are their disaster recovery and business continuity solutions?
- How easily can we terminate this agreement; and how portable is our data?

Cloud-sourced solutions still need to satisfy the requirements of a business case, as a traditional outsourced system would. Whereas past practices would have been to engage in protracted negotiations to develop a customized contract, the current practice is to sign up on the vendors' standardized paper. To calm the practitioners' reflexive discomfort with this approach, it helps to have worked up some minimum parameters (for example, by developing a policy based on responses to the questions above), in which the cloud solution needs to fit so that decisions can be made quickly and with a degree of comfort that taking the standardized, non-negotiated route has not jeopardized the customer's interests.

For example, it is more productive for the practitioner to focus on the number and quality of standards with which the cloud solution complies or the certifications the provider has, rather than trying to negotiate customized contract terms. For example, many managed services providers now comply with the Unified Certification Standard (UCS), which is a certification and audit (similar to a SAS70 audit) for the cloud computing and managed services industry. It is a certification process validated by a third-party accounting firm and a report on the managed services providers' performance can be provided with existing and prospective clients to give neutral, industry accepted assurances where lawyers would have otherwise negotiated customized terms.

Another area in which the old outsourcing ways clash with the new cloud sourcing paradigm is in product features and functionality. Given that a cloud solution provider will develop and release new product features based on industry-wide feedback (especially the large public cloud providers) and to its entire customer base, it no longer makes sense for the customer to be directing what features and functionality should be built into the solution. It does, however, make sense to ask a cloud provider to commit to service roadmaps, which will most likely be aligned with that provider's interests.

The risks that a standard, one-size-fits-all cloud provider's contract poses will, naturally, depend on the function that the provider is to perform, as well as the downside risks if they fail to meet their performance obligations or protect the data entrusted to them. Functions that are not mission-critical, and do not come with significant regulatory commitments such as e-mail, human resources, call center, finance, and back ops, may be good candidates for a simple and streamlined cloud service. In contrast, functions that are closer to the core of your business (if they can be adequately outsourced at all) are good candidates for private-cloud, enhanced-SLA solutions—for an energy company, this may be customer account management, or for a consumer goods company, it could be supply chain management.

Getting into the Cloud

Once you have made the decision to work with a cloud provider, you will need to consider what other contractual impediments stand in your way. For many traditionally outsourced functions, the enterprise may have an incumbent outsourced service provider. As the industry gains sophistication, some providers will be willing and able to break up different responsibilities into a hybrid public/private cloud solution, which can allow more nuanced decision-making. However, for now, these traditional outsourcing arrangements will typically include contractual limitations on the ability to transition from one provider to another, and the offloading process may likewise pose practical or logistical problems. It is important to understand the existing landscape as a part of the broader process of electing a cloud solution.

First, you must understand the outsourcing contract itself. Although rare, some agreements will simply specify fees for early termination. More common is the situation in which an agreement does not spell out an early-termination fee, but instead simply says that the customer may not terminate the agreement without cause during the initial (typically two- to three-year) term of the agreement. In practical terms, this simply means that the customer may not terminate without the provider's consent, which will often come at a negotiated price. When preparing for such a negotiation, consider how much of your business will truly be transitioned from the incumbent provider to the cloud solution: if the functions to be handled by the cloud vendor are part of a larger bundle of services, it may be possible to reduce the total services consumed under the contract without amending it (for instance, by a RRC[10] mechanism, in the case of unit pricing).

Another risk that may not be so apparent from the face of the contract is your ability as a customer to "take back" physical hardware, know-how, or intellectual property (IP) that is necessary to transition to a new supplier. Outsourcing agreements frequently provide (in general terms) for the transition away from the provider, but even if the provider is obligated to provide assistance, it pays to think through exactly what goods and information will be needed. Data, too, must be returned: either in a useable form after having been converted by the outgoing provider directly, or provided in a form that allows the cloud provider to carry out the conversion. In both cases, it will be useful to work with the cloud provider to understand its precise requirements before approaching the existing provider.

If an existing outsourcing agreement cannot be terminated, how can the customer take advantage of the cloud provider's pricing? You should work with the contract team to understand exactly what services are currently provided by the incumbent, and consider whether there is room to "fill in" other functions related to the outsourcing arrangement. Because the shift to the cloud has in some cases disaggregated the technology stack—SaaS on top of PaaS on top of IaaS—you may discover that these related functions can nevertheless be provided more efficiently by the cloud provider than internally, and doing so may help to establish a proof of concept for eventually switching to the cloud provider for the entire stack.

Of course, another alternative is to approach the incumbent provider itself about transitioning to a cloud model. Certainly, the seismic shift to decentralized outsourcing models is not news to the incumbents, and they are actively pursuing new initiatives and offerings in this area.[11] These providers already speak the language of price benchmarking and continuous

---

[10] Reduced resource charge.

[11] *See e.g.* Press Release, Capgemini, Capgemini and VMware to Create Business Cloud Orchestration Solutins to Accelerate the Customer Journey Toward IT as a Service, (Jan. 16, 2014), *available at* http://www.capgemini.com/news/capgemini-and-vmware-to-create-business-cloud-orchestration-solutions-to-accelerate-the.

improvement; therefore, they may well be amenable to transitioning your service to a less expensive cloud-based offering.

The More Things Change, the More They Stay the Same

Finally, it is time to negotiate the actual cloud sourcing agreement. Fortunately, many of your instincts from premises-based outsourcing or licensing arrangements still apply in the cloud age. In particular, you should still think about the following contractual provisions when considering a cloud provider:

Service Level Agreements

Almost without a doubt, the most common SLA (service level agreement) in any IT contract is the hosting uptime commitment, and it certainly applies to hosted cloud services. This measure of performance is critical here, since a cloud service that cannot be reached cannot fulfill any of its other performance obligations to the customer. As with hosting providers generally, large outsourcers will have a standard uptime commitment of their own (including precise procedures for determining performance against the SLA) and may be willing to guarantee higher reliability for higher fees. Even smaller providers that do not operate their own servers can pass through the SLAs offered by their own hosting services (although in practice this is typically their ceiling, not their floor).

For other commitments subject to an SLA, the rule for cloud sourcing as well as outsourcing is to understand the specific service to be offered. For processing services, throughput is likely a significant metric; for storage, retrieval times may matter. At a higher level of abstraction, of course, you should also consider the actual operation of the service being outsourced (perhaps through outputs generated or requests fulfilled, or by user satisfaction surveys). Conversely, for "bare cloud" services such as IaaS and PaaS, the customer itself will be supplying the final application; therefore, any SLAs will be limited to technical, rather than user-visible, performance metrics.

Data Protections

As with traditional outsourcing models, compliance cannot be an afterthought. While the market has progressed from the "wild west" that prevailed a decade ago, it is important to carefully review a provider's credentials to ensure that it can back up its compliance claims. If the provider offers customer referrals, consider specifically requesting contacts with similarly regulated entities. As with any other outsourcing solution, it is also important to contract for specific protections where the potential of monetary recovery is insufficient. For example, customers in the pharmaceutical industry and others for whom procedural assurances are vital should insist on strict change control mechanisms, even to the point of opting for private or self-hosted solutions.

Specific regulatory challenges recur regularly in the cloud context across industries. Consider the potential issues posed by cross-border data transfers. The European Union (EU) and Switzerland restrict the processing of their citizens' data in many other jurisdictions, including the United States. For this reason, it is important to understand every location in which the cloud provider may store or use personal data (even in the case of backups or failovers), and any subcontracting entity that may have access to this data. In general, the rule of thumb should be to keep personal data in its country of origin.

Allocation of Third-Party Risks

As with traditional outsourcing contracts, cloud subscribers should expect to be indemnified for most third-party intellectual property infringement claims, as cloud solutions are every bit as patentable as other IT deployment models. As of this writing, for example, the cloud company Rackspace is defending a high-profile suit by a patent assertion entity on behalf of its users. While indemnity obligations should in general always be carved out from aggregate caps on the indemnifying party's liability, this is especially true in the cloud services context, where annual fees (the most common measure of damages) are likely to be significantly lower than those for traditionally outsourced services. Cloud customers should be wary of indemnity exceptions that negate the indemnity "to the extent the alleged infringement resulted from the Customer's actions." In light of *Akamai*,[12] which liberalized rules for "divided infringement," a patent claim may be infringed if a cloud provider practiced some elements itself and induced its customer to perform the others.

---

[12] *Akamai Technologies, Inc. et al. v. Limelight Networks, Inc.*, 692 F.3d 1301(Fed. Cir. 2012) (en banc).

The ordinary complement of additional indemnities (for privacy breaches or loss of confidential information, for example) should also be carried over from the traditional to the cloud outsourcing world.

Termination Provisions

The ability to walk away from an unsatisfactory outsourcing provider is critical, whether the service is provided on a managed or a cloud basis. In the public cloud context, providers may be more willing than traditional, managed service providers to permit termination on short notice (as low as a single billing cycle), because the very nature of a one-size-fits-all system means that the provider does not need to recoup significant start-up or build-out costs. Still, of course, outsourcers are always incentivized to lock customers in to preserve long-term revenue. If a provider refuses to bargain on the minimum term of service, think about the various ways that its performance may fall short of your expectations, and try to build these into the right to terminate for cause. For example, repeated or significant failures to meet SLAs is a common trigger, and any acts or omissions that could have regulatory impacts should be grounds for immediate termination.

In addition to ensuring the contractual right to terminate, be sure to consider the practical ability to transition away from the provider successfully. The first step should be to ask the provider about its offloading process. In many cases, providers think of this final service in terms of a "data dump." If the service to be performed is principally data storage, this may be workable (and in fact ideal); if, however, the provider will be carrying out any significant processing, or will have converted the data to a non-native format, a more nuanced approach will be required. Given that the business relationship with the provider may well have soured by the time the migration is to occur, consider requiring that the provider agree to cooperate with your agents or designated third-party consultants to accomplish the transition. Subject to any regulatory imperatives, it may also make sense to require the provider to retain the data for a set period before certifying its destruction, in case the migration is later found not to have fully succeeded.

Conclusion

One of the biggest disruptive technological forces over the past decade has been the move from "assets to access." The increased prevalence of cloud-based solutions is an example of that force in action. Organizations no longer needs to own assets—data centers, servers, storage space, or applications—to take advantage of high-tech services. Access to the Internet is all that is required, with resources and applications just a click away. This new technology, as with any disruptive force, is as unsettling to incumbents not nimble enough to evolve as it is exciting to consumers desperate to move away from inflexible, monolithic solutions that only ever partially address those consumers' needs.

Practitioners need to be mindful of how to address the inherent tensions between providers and customers around SLAs, intellectual property rights, data protection and security, amendments to service or product features and termination and service transition concerns. The trend suggests that different models are evolving for different cloud services—for example the allocation of risk and responsibility between vendor and customer in a PaaS agreement will not likely make sense for a SaaS-based solution. However, all parties are starting to rely on adopting industry standards and certifications to define behavior that would otherwise be heavily negotiated between parties. Over time, cloud-based solutions will become the obvious choice and practitioners will look back on our current trepidations with wonder. Right now, assuming vendors and customers find the right service model and risk mitigation strategies, cloud-based solutions are and can be a good choice for specific elements of the stack, and eventually, all of it.

Key Takeaways

- Advise clients that once they have made the decision to work with a cloud provider, they will need to consider what other contractual impediments stand in their way. They should also ensure that they understand the outsourcing contract itself.

- Negotiating the actual cloud sourcing agreement entails focusing on service legal agreement terms. Understand the specific service to be offered. For processing services, throughput is likely a significant metric; for storage, retrieval times may matter. Consider the actual operation of the service being outsourced.

- Carefully review a provider's credentials to ensure that it can back up its compliance claims. Consider specifically requesting contacts with similarly regulated entities. Contract for specific protections where the potential of monetary recovery is insufficient. Understand every location in which the cloud provider may store or use personal data, and any subcontracting entity that may have access to this data.

- Expect to be indemnified for most third-party intellectual property infringement claims, as cloud solutions are every bit as patentable as other IT deployment models.

- Ensure the contractual right to terminate, and be sure to consider the practical ability to transition away from the provider successfully. Ask the provider about its offloading process. Require the provider to retain the data for a set period before certifying its destruction, in case the migration is later found not to have fully succeeded.

Emma Maconick is a partner on the ccorporate team in King & Spalding's Palo Alto, California office. She has in-depth experience of a broad range of intellectual property and technology transactions, which vary from sophisticated cross-border deals for multi-national corporations, institutional lenders, venture capitalists and private equity funds to discrete development, commercialization and licensing agreements for start-ups, emerging companies, R&D entities and universities.

Ms. Maconick has extensive transactional experience across three continents advising clients on IT outsourcing transactions, across a broad range of business processes such as co-location, finance and accounting, facilities management, network security, application development and maintenance. She often assists clients on large-scale, complex outsourcing transactions in a variety of industry sectors, including in the financial, health care, consumer goods, energy and information security industries. Ms. Maconick's practice involves delivering business-oriented solutions to complicated IP and IT asset management issues arising in product research, development and deployment strategies; procurement and supply agreements; software, hosting, outsourcing, big data and cloud-based services; platform and infrastructure agreements; privacy policies and Internet commerce-related agreements.

Acknowledgment: *With thanks to Bill Roche, partner, King & Spalding and Daniel Ray, associate, King & Spalding for their editorial oversight.*

Structuring Multi-Supplier IT Environments

Dr. Trevor W. Nagel

Partner

White & Case LLP

ASPATORE

Introduction: Move to Multi-Supplier IT Environments

The sourcing landscape is rapidly changing: larger enterprises are moving away from monolithic, single supplier outsourcing arrangements. For a host of reasons, this single sourced information technology (IT) model that dominated the outsourcing market for its first two decades is no longer the paradigm for large, complex corporations. First and foremost, large outsourcing suppliers generally did not handle effectively or show adequate flexibility as major changes occurred in customers' IT environments or businesses. While the major IT suppliers have generally handled large-scale processing and storage and mid-range operations effectively and in most cases remained involved in customer IT environments as members of the emerging multi-supplier panels, most enterprise customers have recognized that to obtain expertise and nimbleness across a range of service offerings, they must align service outsourcings to supplier competencies and chose "best of breed" in each service area. For example, there is an increasing need to redesign and rethink IT platforms and how they operate in an increasingly mobile world involving a diverse set of suppliers. Moreover, the more global and diversified a large enterprise's footprint, the more unlikely that a single supplier can provide the same level of service across a range of IT functions everywhere in the world. Thus, the IT needs, and the portfolio mix of suppliers, may be similar but are not identical across the different geographical hubs of an organization.

The move to a multi-supplier IT environment has also been influenced by recent economic factors. The monolithic, single supplier deals were often long-term deals in which a duration of seven to even ten years was not unusual. Despite most of these arrangements including price adjustment provisions based upon benchmarks, customers often became highly frustrated at the fact that they were locked into prices that consistently took considerable time to adjust and, even when adjusted, were above what they believed they could obtain in the market. To a large degree, this was a product of the problematic nature of benchmarking for large and especially global operations. Their IT services, systems, and networks were rarely "standard" so there were not ready "comparables." It was difficult and time-consuming to obtain sufficient and reliable benchmarks that enabled price adjustments to occur in accordance with what was happening in the market. This issue became all the more exacerbated at times of economic downturn when suppliers, often based on technological advances or more efficient employment of existing technologies, would offer significantly lower rates in new deals.

In addition, the marketplace had become more competitive early last decade. One factor was that the Indian IT vendors, who had founded their businesses upon rendering ADM services, expanded operations into a broader range of IT processing and storage offerings. There was also the emergence of regional IT suppliers in the Americas, the European Union, and the Asia-Pacific regions. Then came the emergence of a set of disruptive IT providers such as Amazon and Rackspace. The accumulative effect of these trends was that large-scale enterprises no longer wanted to be locked into long term arrangements with a single supplier but were procuring IT services on shorter term agreements, often of three- to five-years duration, dividing their needs across a variety of suppliers who could offer the best value and solutions for the corresponding sets of services or platforms. In today's economic climate, recovering from the global economic crisis of 2008, value for money is only more critical. We stress that best value should be viewed not only in terms of price, solution and service quality but also in terms of a supplier's willingness and ability to adapt to fast-changing needs in the more mobile contemporary technology and business world.

To take an example, a multinational retail corporation entered into a long-term monolithic sourcing arrangement early last decade to provide IT services structured around a global network of mega-stores. Two-thirds of the way into the ten-year arrangement, the retail corporation concluded that this deal was no longer meeting its business needs. Pricing was opaque and inelastic, service levels lagged industry benchmarks. But even more importantly, the supplier was unwilling or unable to change quickly and meet new business requirements in the customer's increasingly competitive and dynamic market. Significant purchasing was shifting from in-store sales to a variety of on-line channels. The retail corporation concluded that the lack of alignment between IT and business either hindered launching new services and products to market at all or on a time line that was necessary to keep up with market demand and competitors. They embarked on a far-reaching transformation of their IT function and supply base. The foundation of this restructuring was a decision to re-source its IT services in a multi-supplier, "best of breed" model. We applied best practices for advanced governance in a multi-supplier IT environment for these series of sourcings as discussed later.

A further influence upon the trend to multi-supplier environments is the growth of both cloud computing and as a service (aaS) delivery models. Underlying both of these movements is the establishment of IT standards. To be able to plug quickly into the processing and storage capabilities of a cloud provider, or to utilize other aaS cloud products, systems have to work off a common set of standards. Similarly, when a supplier is combining various products and services into a single coordinated offering such as infrastructure as a service (IaaS), this fusion of IT requires agreement within the technology community as to what standards will apply to enable the final products to operate in a consistent, seamless manner with a common level of quality. This increase in standardization necessary to participate in a cloud or to fully utilize aaS offerings results in IT environments where it is relatively easy to integrate the services of different suppliers or to substitute suppliers in situations of poor service, poor price or unmet changing needs.

Cloud computing has also had a significant impact on the pricing of contemporary sourcing transactions. Cloud computing has driven more agile, on-demand commercial models. Rather than being locked-in to large long-term deals with significant management fees, minimum purchase requirements and "penalties" if terminated early for convenience, the broader market is moving toward "utility" models where fees are more consumption-based and where there is a greater ease to switch suppliers if a better or cheaper offering is available. Although still an evolving field and determining pricing models in both a cloud or aaS environment is still somewhat problematic, the trending is clear as corporations see the advantages of more transparent, cost-effective and flexible IT services. But note that these models are all made possible by the underlying trend toward multi-supplier IT environments.

In fact, the outcome of the common theme of dissatisfaction with the monolithic, sole-supplier model of the past is not the search for a better and more responsive single supplier but the move to a multi-supplier environment. All of these trends and developments are combining in such a way that, for the enterprise to take full advantage of the promise of these IT innovations, a multi-supplier IT environment is the only alternative. But this multi-supplier environment is not without its challenges. First it is imperative that both the enterprise and its strategic suppliers recognize the importance of developing a sophisticated integration function for combining various supplier and often internal inputs into coordinated value-added products and services for both internal and the corporation's ultimate customers. This requires the sourcing lawyers and other deal makers to have a solid grasp not only of the transaction at hand but the complete supply chain or "cloud" landscape of which that deal is but an element. This integration function is discussed in the next section. Second, "governance" has been a catchphrase for a while in the IT industry but there is now real competitive advantage in developing more sophisticated and transparent frameworks which anticipate likely friction points among parties, align the supplier's incentives with the customer's business objectives and explicitly address collaboration among strategic suppliers to develop the optimal IT solutions. Best practices in governance of a multi-supplier IT environment will be disclosed later. Finally, there is the need to recognize that this is organizational change of a magnitude that has often not been contemplated by the chief information officer (CIO), the IT function or the sourcing lawyers who advise on structuring these complex sourcing worlds. We will touch on the changing role of the CIO in a later section.

Emergence of the Services Integration Role

One consequence of moving to a multi-supplier IT environment is that there is an opportunity—or even a need—to reassess who plays the services integration role. To ensure end-to-end service integration among the portfolio of suppliers, it is necessary to design and implement the technology and to manage, measure, and orchestrate a diverse set of service offerings. Previously in the largely single-sourced model, the monolithic IT supplier was the integrator, coordinating and packing services for consumption by the enterprise. In moving to a multi-sourced IT environment, either the customer or one of the strategic suppliers must assume this role to avoid any inefficiency or confusion among the other suppliers. This question is sometimes not even considered in migrating to multi-supplier environments and requires the allocation of decision rights among the strategic suppliers.

For both economic reasons and so the corporation has the best perspective on its IT requirements and how they are constantly changing, this integration role increasingly will be assumed by the customer. This may require the enterprise to staff, build, and implement an IT service management (ITSM) competence and systems with related processes such as databases. To demonstrate the level of complexity with databases alone, the finance industry now has to monitor its accounts on a global basis to comply with "know your customer" regulations in an age of anti-money laundering and tax evasion, yet still conform with disparate national privacy and data protection laws.

A corporate function that has outsourced many operations is no longer just administering the services being delivered by its IT suppliers but is more directly involved in the stream of service delivery, product architecture and product definition. This is a markedly different role than that played by traditional vendor management offices (VMO). It can lead to greater efficiencies if structured properly. As one example, when the customer takes on the services integration role and couples that with advanced multi-supplier governance, which among other things provides the suppliers greater knowledge of what is happening in the customer's environment, there are significantly more opportunities to reduce duplication of effort or other inefficiencies or even to innovate.

This ever-increasing march toward cost optimization is not just about "shaving the nickel off the price of a paperclip"; it is a value proposition. Over the last five to ten years, companies have been taking a closer look at their peers and disruptive players coming into their markets, in particular cost-income ratios, and feeling even greater pressures to reduce expenditure. Increasingly, IT is no longer viewed solely as a support function but as a strategic component of a business delivering services to customers. Instead of saying "I run a network," the more enlightened CIOs are declaring, "I deliver communications and IT-enhanced products to my internal business customers." In other words, they are striving to integrate themselves in a more direct way into the corporation's business strategy development and the design and delivery of the products and services offered to the corporation's ultimate customers. And this requires forward thinking CIOs to understand how the IT environment operates at all levels and integrates a portfolio of services and products to generate seamless offerings.

Best Practices for a Multi-Supplier IT Environment

The move to multi-supplier, "best of breed" IT environments has generated a set of best practices to address this very different IT model. To a large extent, the best practices in the sole-sourced outsourcing world were focused around optimizing the price-performance ratio for a service. To that end, the VMO was focused on clear and unambiguous definition of service levels, ensuring that the levels were met and regularly adjusting the prices of services to reflect the current market. To a large extent, these practices evolved to optimize the existing supplier relationship as migrating to another vendor was a major, time-consuming and costly undertaking with no assurance on enhanced performance. With increased standardization necessary to operate a multi-supplier IT environment and shorter-term contractual arrangements, there are new more agile, on-demand commercial models that enable a relatively expeditious substitution of suppliers in the event that there is a better or cheaper version of the same standardized service.

Many of the emerging best practices for a multi-supplier environment relate to orchestrating suppliers to integrate the services and solutions that meet the ever-changing needs of the internal business customers and, in turn, the corporation's ultimate customers. In other words, there has been a need to redefine the roles of enterprise customer and supplier in a multi-supplier environment and develop practices that drive cooperation among all involved that is critical to developing these integrated products. As is often said, the aaS movement has broken down or "clouded" the traditional distinction between vendor and customer (whereas in the traditional sourcing model this distinction was unequivocal). aaS offerings enable the enterprise customer to fold both its data and unique systems into the end product, rendering the distinction between customer and supplier no longer as clear as it once was. And when these aaS offerings are extended into the corporation's own end-user and customer base, another level of integration and blurring can occur. It is necessary to carefully review and analyze how the corporation is integrating its own proprietary information and services with those from its suppliers, and then how that package is passed on to its own end-users and customers, for sourcing lawyers to advise properly on the liabilities and risks associated with these aaS offerings.

A key best practice for managing multiple suppliers in the contemporary IT environment is structuring and implementing a sophisticated panel governance regime. The panel governance regime should govern IT operations at multiple levels both within the enterprise customer and as between the supplier and the customer (whereas traditional models focused only on one level and only between the supplier and customer), and should drive coordination and cooperative behavior among the customer and its strategic suppliers. Governing a complex, multi-supplier IT environment is time-consuming, requires a different skill set (than traditional VMOs) and incurs transaction costs. Accordingly, it is important for the enterprise to determine who are the strategic suppliers who need to address a broader range of issues and need to work together to develop and deliver solutions. A related question is how many strategic suppliers to include in the panel governance arrangement. At one extreme, a literal approach to "best of breed" is to select the single supplier who best provides each individual service. In a complex IT environment, this could be a large number of suppliers and managing a panel of that size could in itself become a major problem and cost. In addition, it is necessary to recognize that sophisticated panel governance is also a significant cost for the strategic suppliers. They are unlikely to play the roles required, in particular the roles that take them beyond the four corners of their sourcing agreement, unless their involvement with the enterprise is of such a dimension that warrants that level of commitment and involvement.

Although there is no hard and fast answer to how many strategic suppliers should be on the panel, two "rules of thumb" have emerged. First, as the time and effort to govern the environment increases with each additional supplier, careful scrutiny should be paid to any decision to have more than four or five strategic suppliers. This usually means that the strategic suppliers are each combining together and delivering a number of IT services and products. Again, it is necessary to consider carefully what are the optimal "bundles" of services and products in the particular IT environment in order that each strategic supplier can best leverage its strengths and capabilities and cooperate effectively with other suppliers. Second, each supplier requires at a minimum a set of services that aggregate to approximately ten percent of the value of services in the IT environment. If a strategic supplier is providing less than this figure, there is a serious question as to whether it will be sufficiently involved from both an economic and engagement perspective in the whole IT environment to play an effective and committed role on the panel.

Underpinning this panel governance system for strategic suppliers is an over-arching framework arrangement. Best practices dictate that this is an agreement that all strategic suppliers *and the corporation* execute. It is distinct from and "sits above" the individual customer-supplier service contracts, governing the way all parties, including the corporation, work together. This framework governance agreement changes the role of the corporation; it is no longer a traditional "hub and spoke" governance model, where the customer is in the middle "directing traffic" between suppliers. Instead, it establishes a governance structure led by the corporation in which all parties participate. In this regard, it also changes the role of the customer, placing the customer "on the same level" as the suppliers. This reflects there are two performances in a complex services arrangement: the performance of services by the suppliers and the performance of obligations by the customer, including the key services integration role. There are a number of important questions relating to this services integration function. For example, is it technology, process, or data driven? What aspects of integration should be retained by the customer and what should be undertaken by one or more of the suppliers? How is the integration function monitored, reported, and managed? Does it require a skill set beyond that traditionally found in the IT world, whether on the customer or supplier side? These are all questions to be resolved through the panel governance process. In addition, note that this integration role has consequences up the "value chain" as savvy CIOs have used this opportunity as a catalyst to help redefine their role from the "back office" to "sitting at the table" with the heads of key business units because the development of products and services for its own customers is now inextricably intertwined with technology.

It is essential that this governance framework agreement drives cooperation among the strategic suppliers, both to resolve problems collectively and to innovate and improve the IT environment to meet the corporation's enterprise-wide business objectives. As many of the strategic suppliers are now undertaking managerial functions and roles that were historically part of the internal corporation, it is important that they do not just focus on the delivery of contracted services but think about how those services can be changed or more integrated effectively with the services provided by other suppliers and better to meet the corporation's emerging objectives and enterprise-wide goals. These cooperative and collaborative behaviors do not come naturally to a group of suppliers who directly compete with one another. The suppliers must be incentivized to do so. First, this can be achieved through new and innovative service levels measured across *all* of them—coordination indicia—that award bonuses or assess credits according to how effectively they cooperate. Second, these behaviors can also be driven by being offered opportunities to expand their business with the customer. Most complex enterprise IT environments have a constant stream of new projects which can be used to reward these strategic suppliers, particularly as they come to understand better the corporation's goals and objectives and how the enterprise operates. In other words, the more sophisticated suppliers see effective panel governance regimes as an "oligopoly" for future projects and initiatives: namely, a long-term relationship with the enterprise and thus, a positive development.

The corporation also benefits from the ongoing contestability resulting from the suppliers wanting new work to be distributed among the panel members rather than being put out to bid in the open market. There are reduced transaction costs and the allocation of projects among panel members generally results in a quicker time to market. If a new project is not meeting schedule or budget, it can more easily be opened up to other panel members given they are already under contract and have familiarity of the customer and its IT environment. Moreover, if any supplier is deficient in its performance of services, the other panel members generally are already familiar with how these services should be provided in that IT environment. Thus, migration of services between panelists can be undertaken expeditiously and with minimum business interruption. This is particularly the case if the sourcing arrangements for strategic suppliers are all on a same modular, "plug-n-play" contract structure, which is another best practice of mature multi-supplier IT environments.

Finally, a sophisticated panel governance scheme needs to be tailored to fit the enterprise's objectives and IT environment. In other words, there is not a "one size fits all" solution to this ongoing governance issue. The governance structure has to be seen to be a "living" operation that needs to be sufficiently flexible to adjust to the changes in the technology, commercial and external economic environments. The best practice is to design the governance framework agreement to deal initially with the transition issues when migrating from the monolithic, sole-sourced to the new multi-supplier target environment. In most circumstances, this will involve developing a route map for bringing on suppliers over time with a roll out of services that will need to be governed and integrated as the environment is transformed. It is important to understand that that the transition and operational go-live phases will be significantly different for each supplier, a lesson that will probably sustain throughout the relationship. Moreover, any sourcing arrangement dealing with a complex and dynamic environment cannot be prescriptive in nature and must contemplate ongoing change. Any changes that are known at the time of executing the deal, and any friction points that have been identified during the procurement process, should be built into the design of the governance regime at the outset.

It should be noted that an issue might have several facets at different levels in the IT environment. For example, there may be operational issues in terms of how the services are integrated together (in some instances, delivery of services may be from one supplier to another supplier) but there are probably also more overarching strategic concerns regarding how the services are integrated to meet a business unit's and, in the long run, ultimate end-users' concerns. This latter set of issues is very important as aaS offerings evolve. It is critical that the governance system addresses these different levels of operation and makes certain that the right information and data is supplied to those among the strategic suppliers and the enterprise who are managing these concerns. There also needs to be mechanisms by which the suppliers can be continually informed as to potential developments in both the enterprise and, correspondingly, in the IT environment. Reciprocally, there should be mechanisms enabling the enterprise customer to learn, and potentially to influence, how suppliers are evolving their own services and products.

In the past, the VMO was often charged with managing large sourcing or enterprise-wide IT arrangements. Over time, the dynamic and ever changing nature of these long-term sourcing arrangements led to a recognition that optimizing these relationships was more than simply confirming that contractual obligations and service levels were being met.

Thus, more sophisticated management mechanisms have begun to emerge, albeit somewhat slowly. The advent of multi-supplier worlds have resulted in major enterprises recognizing that governance is not just a nice "touch" but essential to running these complex IT environments that are constantly in flux. Pointedly, this is governance rather than contract management. As suppliers play more and more the roles that were once internal to an organization, not only do the conversations with them have to take place simultaneously at different levels but also the suppliers must be in dialogue with each other in ways that benefit and advance the enterprise.

The achievement of enterprise-wide goals requires that the corporation have a relationship at least with the major strategic suppliers that extends beyond the "four corners" of the mere contracts at hand. The challenges of these multi-supplier IT environments are such that the measure of a successful sourcing transaction is not the quality of the contracts upon execution but rather the status of the transaction after day 1,000 of the term. This is a test as to whether the contractual framework was sufficiently flexible to enable the parties to evolve the services in a way that meets changing enterprise objectives in what often is a quite different business environment than that when the contracts were signed. The governance framework agreement and related panel governance tools are key facilitators of the most important aspect of these complex long-term service arrangements: the delivery of services that meet the ever-changing business requirements over time.

Changing Role of the CIO, the IT Function and the Sourcing Lawyer

A major theme of this migration from the monolithic, sole-sourced outsourcing arrangement to a multi-supplier IT environment is that it involves substantial organizational change at many levels for many players. The integration role that is now being performed by the enterprise is a significant change in itself and often requires the infusion of skill sets that were not present in the enterprise in the traditional sourcing model. To take but one example, it requires the enterprise to have IT executives who can interact with and orchestrate suppliers in a way that modifies their service offerings to generate a better, more holistic outcome rather than just confirming that suppliers are meeting a set of pre-determined service levels. This governance role has a portfolio perspective; it is essential to ensure that no IT project is operating in "its own space" and that all services and products are aligned at the operational and more importantly, the value-add levels. If the governance framework agreement is generating collaboration between the major strategic suppliers, it is necessary to be able to monitor and direct that collaboration to optimize the outcome for the enterprise. In other words, those running the information technology service management systems at the enterprise are playing a significantly more pro-active role than just responding to the performance being undertaken by the suppliers. They are providing a performance themselves and it is important that it drives the suppliers to understand better the goals of enterprise and to interact in a productive manner.

At the highest level, there is a changing role for the CIO. The CIO was once an IT executive whose primary concern was whether the corporation's IT system was up and running and performing to the service levels designated in the outsourcing agreements. That has changed dramatically in the multi-supplier IT environment. Not only is the CIO now responsible for the services of its strategic suppliers being integrated to achieve optimal performance but also ensuring that these services are aligned with the business needs of the enterprise. This role requires not just dealing with the suppliers, but also interacting with key business unit executives. Given the degree to which technology is an integral part of many of the enterprise products, it is necessary for the CIO to be "sitting at the table" with key business executives as plans for new products are developing. The IT services portfolio must be synched with the enterprise objectives. This is a significant change for the CIO from that systems operations role of the past.

The cloud has also played a role in changing this function. Product development in the cloud can reduce what were frequently, for example in the finance industry, ninety to 120-day cycles to a process that can be completed in a matter of days. This often involves the IT function working hand-in-hand with the business units to determine the optimal cloud environment and setting up test and development sites to meet the business needs. If the CIO and the IT function are to play this role more effectively, it is important that the CIO encourage the major strategic suppliers to think of themselves as integral parts of this process. And this is organizational change for the suppliers as well. Gone are the days when a supplier just inserted a delivery team to meet its "hard" service level obligations.

It is always difficult to predict exactly what an enterprise's future IT needs would be and the suppliers need to understand this. Therefore, it is important that the suppliers are "on board" with structuring flexible arrangements that can be scaled to meet either an increase or decrease in demand. For that reason, more enlightened CIOs are demanding utility or aaS "pay-as-you-go" pricing systems. For example, if a corporation develops a new product, product line or business unit whose sales increase dramatically, or if it engages in the acquisition or sale of a business unit, it is important to not be impeded by an inflexible, fixed price commercial model of the past where there was little or no transparency or leverage. The utility-based pricing of cloud offerings provides the agility for enterprise to pay for the processing and storage it requires as business needs change, often in a dramatic fashion over short durations.

This need for transparency also has implications in other ways as the IT function deals with its strategic suppliers through the panel governance regime. In a fast changing and dynamic world, it is important that the strategic suppliers are constantly informed as to how the environment, and in turn the portfolio of services, may be changing and their advice should be sought on how to deal optimally with those emerging requirements. In many cases, the CIO may not know exactly what is required or the degree to which demands for those services will change. It is important to develop a governance regime in which parties can be open with each other, including the strategic suppliers among themselves, to best fashion solutions to meet the enterprise's needs. One of the advantages of having several major players on a panel is the wealth of knowledge and experience they possess dealing with similar situations across a range of circumstances. As one CIO recently stated, "I want the best from my top two or three suppliers meeting with me to come up with the best solutions to my challenges and problems." That requires transparency and a collaborative ethos.

The role of the outsourcing lawyer has also changed in this multi-supplier IT environment. The sourcing lawyer is often the prime source for best practices concerning the structure and content of the governance framework agreement. The sourcing lawyer should not seem just a resource for drafting a set of outsourcing terms and conditions, together with a service level agreement and associated credits. The sourcing lawyer is now having to consider coordination indices and the quantification of other portfolio governance components that will encourage the suppliers to work collaboratively in a specific and often unique environment. The sourcing lawyer needs to develop a set of "constitutional" provisions to set up a framework for resolving the inevitable ongoing issues and disputes that may not have been contemplated at the time that the framework governance agreement was executed. There is a role for the sourcing lawyer beyond the execution of the basic services agreements and that role is more affirmative than providing litigation counsel when impasses arise. In a complex IT environment or aaS offering, unpacking the process may be a very costly option and result in significant business discontinuity. The sourcing lawyer must provide the mechanisms that enable everyday disputes to be resolved before they fester into impasses or, at a minimum, to structure the whole IT environment contractual arrangement in a plug-n-play manner that substitution of one supplier for another is a relatively easy outcome.

Conclusion

The sourcing landscape is a very different world as these large scale enterprises enter their second and third generation of services arrangements. Services arrangements are now occurring at multiple levels throughout the organization and involve a degree of integration that makes demands upon costs, service efficiency and customer satisfaction in a manner that neither the enterprise nor the strategic suppliers previously contemplated. With the increased diversity in the requests for IT services, the growth of cloud computing and IaaS and other aaS offerings, and increasing sophistication of platforms, often as platform as a service, there are many IT suppliers—traditional and disruptive—with a set of competencies that can change dramatically how an enterprise achieves its objectives and goals. And the corporate IT function is no longer focused on a VMO just administering these service arrangements and managing to service levels being met. The corporate IT function is more and more playing a vital services integration role and is a pro-active part of putting together this diverse range of services in the optimal fashion to meet the enterprise's ever-changing objectives and goals. This more complex, multi-supplier IT environment demands a robust and highly tailored portfolio governance strategy, the capstone of which is a sophisticated panel governance system for the enterprise and its strategic suppliers to explore and deliver upon these possibilities.

Key Takeaways

Multi-supplier IT environments are fast becoming the norm at the enterprise-level. Among steps enterprise customers should consider when structuring a multi-supplier IT environment are:

- Determine whether and to what extent the customer should play the services integration role, and structure systems, IT processes and sourcing contracts that are aligned with that function.

- Discern who are the key strategic suppliers and establish a sophisticated, multi-supplier governance structure and processes to manage those relationships on an ongoing basis at multiple levels.

- Develop and implement a governance framework agreement by and between the customer and strategic suppliers that breaks down barriers to, and drives behaviors through incentives for, suppliers to cooperate, collaborate and innovate to meet the enterprise's objectives.

- Establish where applicable supplier panels utilizing modular, plug 'n play contract structures to drive flexibility and ongoing contestability.

- Recognize the changing role of the CIO, the IT function and the lawyers advising them in contemporary, multi-supplier IT environments.

Dr. Trevor W. Nagel, a partner with White & Case LLP, is the chair of the Global Sourcing and Technology Transactions Group and is based in Washington, DC. He represents clients in North America, Europe, and Asia, advising on legal and business issues relating to sourcing and complex procurement transactions. His practice focuses on structuring, negotiating, and implementing information technology, offshore application development and management, managed network services and business process outsourcing transactions, joint ventures, strategic alliances and co-marketing arrangements.

Dr. Nagel concentrates on establishing sustainable sourcing relationships that accommodate the changes and challenges that inevitably arise in long-term arrangements. He stresses the client's entire operating environment, with an emphasis on the critical (though often ignored) integration issues that are present in any multi-source situation. He has extensive experience structuring collaborative governance frameworks that anticipate likely friction points and align supplier incentives with client objectives. He has also worked on some of the larger cloud computing initiatives at the enterprise-level. He is regarded as a leading outsourcing lawyer by top publications such as Chambers *and* Legal 500. *He was awarded first place for this work by the* Financial Times *in the US Legal Innovation Awards 2013 for the "Lawyers to the Innovators" category in recognition of his innovation and thought leadership regarding governance in complex multi-supplier environments. He was also named by* Financial Times *as one of the "Top Ten Agents for Change."*

Acknowledgment: *Dr. Trevor W. Nagel would like to thank Mr. Robert E. L. Hasty, counsel with White & Case LLP, for his assistance with this chapter.*

Robert E. L. Hasty, counsel with White & Case LLP, is in the Sourcing and Technology Transactions Group and is based in Washington, DC. He advises clients on legal and business issues in sourcing, other complex technology-centric arrangements, and the IT/IP aspects of M&A transactions. He has negotiated transactions across North America, Europe, the Middle East, South Africa and Asia-Pac. With over twenty years of sourcing experience, he has advised clients in an array of industries on virtually all aspects of IT and business process outsourcing. His practice also focuses on strategic alliances and joint ventures, IP development and exploitation, and telecommunications services and systems integration agreements. Mr. Hasty has a keen understanding of multinational arrangements, having spent approximately forty percent of his career negotiating cross-border agreements in other countries.

Mr. Hasty is a recognized leader in his field, including being ranked in Chambers USA *and* Legal 500 *for technology and outsourcing. He was awarded first place by the* Financial Times *in the US Legal Innovation Awards 2013 for the "Lawyers to the Innovators" category in recognition of his innovation and thought leadership regarding governance in complex multi-supplier environments.*

Key Contract Considerations and Governance Issues for Managing Outsourcing Risks

Michael Orlando

Partner

Sheppard Mullin Richter & Hampton LLP

ASPATORE

Managing Risks

Risks and challenges vary widely depending on the type of outsourcing relationship and industry. The risks also increase when the outsourcing relationship is offshore rather than within the United States. Some of the common risks that companies face in outsourcing are decreased quality, performance failures, increased lead or delivery times, intellectual property ownership, misappropriation of intellectual property, data and privacy security, and regulatory compliance.

There are various ways to address these types of risks, all of which start with advance planning. Selecting the right service provider and conducting proper due diligence is key. Clients should, if possible, go through a proper request for proposal (RFP) process to select the best outsource providers. Sometimes this is not possible due to budgets, time constraints, or the uniqueness of the product or service being outsourced, but selecting the right outsource provider is very important. When clients are forced to use a certain service provider because they have a deadline and do not have time for a proper RFP process or to conduct the appropriate due diligence, these risks become even greater. Other important factors to diligence when considering an outsource provider are the financial strength of the service provider, if it has the ability to scale as the company grows, if it regularly upgrades or plans to upgrade its equipment and technology, and whether it has essential recovery and back-up plans. Due diligence may also need to extend to the subcontractors of the outsourcing partner. In software as a service (SaaS) and other cloud-based service contracts, it is very common for the outsource provider to rely on other subcontractors that provide the hosting facilities, network infrastructure, and hardware and software platforms. In many cases, the software as a service company will only be passing through the service levels from its hosting company when agreeing to up-time guarantees; however, companies need to be careful that they do not overlook those aspects of the service levels that are within the service provider's control. Companies need to ask the right questions about how the outsourcing provider is itself outsourcing critical components of the service.

Once the outsource provider has been properly vetted, some risks can still arise. Risks associated with poor performance or disagreements about the scope of work can happen in any outsourcing arrangement. Therefore, it is key to make sure a framework is in place to reduce these risks or to identify and deal with them before they become big problems. The master services agreement (MSA) can be a valuable tool in mitigating these risks by properly documenting the scope of work, change-control processes, required service levels, service level credits, remedies, indemnification, and providing for a management, reporting, audit, and review structure to govern the relationship and ensure greater transparency.

Using an offshore provider increases many of these risks because of the introduction of political risks in countries with less stable governments, less-protective laws, or currency risks associated with weaker economies. For example, Ukraine has become a popular outsourcing destination for software development and IT services in the past few years, but recent internal political unrest and the conflict with Russia over Crimea demonstrate why properly assessing risks when dealing with foreign service providers is so important. There is also greater risk of miscommunication from language and cultural barriers. US law can add additional regulation to companies offshoring their services with Foreign Corrupt Practices Act (FCPA) compliance, labor law issues, export and import regulations, and customs clearance risks. Intellectual property risks also increase in certain countries where infringement and misappropriation are common and where intellectual property rights enforcement is difficult.

Some risks are greater when keeping functions in house, while others are diminished. Depending on the company's in-house capabilities, it may benefit from outsourcing certain functions. For example, HR outsourcing is extremely common because of the ever-changing labor laws and employment taxes. It may be less risky to outsource this function from a regulatory risk perspective, provided the service provider has a good track record of keeping up with regulatory changes and related upgrades to its systems to account for these changes in an accurate and timely manner. It may also be far too costly and time-consuming for a company to develop certain functions in-house. On the flip side, when it comes to protecting intellectual property, it is far less risky to keep intellectual property development functions in-house, or to at least keep core intellectual property development in-house and outsource non-critical pieces. Many risks also become greater when outsourcing because of the loss of total control of quality and timely performance.

Managing Data Security Risks

In information technology (IT) and business process outsourcing (BPO), companies are expending an ever-increasing amount of resources to protect sensitive consumer data and manage the risks of potential security breaches. In the past few years, IT outsourcing and BPO have become increasingly cloud based, leading to more consumer data being transmitted and stored in the cloud. Privacy and data security are becoming increasingly sensitive for companies outsourcing services that involve personal information. Privacy and data security fears are also becoming increasingly sensitive topics as the public becomes more aware of the large amount of personal data freely given on a daily basis to companies and the risks associated with that data being stored in the ubiquitous cloud. News headlines about the 2013 holiday season security breach at Target, the NSA leak by Edward Snowden, and similar stories have resulted in calls for additional privacy and security legislation. State and federal government agencies such as the Federal Trade Commission (FTC) have increased their enforcement efforts.

The privacy and data security issues for business-to-consumer companies that outsource their IT generally differ from more regulated industries such as financial services, health care, and education. The types and levels of personal information collected, transmitted, and stored by these regulated industries is much greater, and the regulatory liability is higher. The current trend is that more stringent industry-based regulations are becoming frequent and being applied more broadly to those involved in the outsourcing relationship. Legislators believe that more needs to be done to protect sensitive personal data and that greater enforcement and increased penalties for violations will lead to better safety measures. For example, the new Health Insurance Portability and Accountability Act of 1996 (HIPAA) rules that went into effect in 2013 expanded the types of outsource providers subject to HIPAA to providers of data transmission services that involve protected health information. As a result, health care IT providers of all types are now required to comply with HIPAA. The health care providers themselves are now having to ensure that a greater number of their outsource providers are in compliance and now face great liability under the new rules. Service providers that before were exempt from HIPAA's requirements now must enter into HIPAA-compliant "business associate" agreements, as required by law.

The regulatory environment has a profound impact on the types and level of risk associated with outsourcing. The regulatory and legal compliance risks obviously increase in highly regulated industries. IT outsourcing relationships in industries that deal with sensitive personal information such as banking, health care, and education also face higher regulatory scrutiny and oversight, with higher fines and liability if they are not in compliance with applicable law. All companies dealing with information subject to regulation will need to ensure that the provider has gone through regulatory compliance audits, has proper procedures and policies in place to ensure its personnel comply with regulations, has proper training for its personnel on a regular basis, and understands the company's risk for non-compliance. Companies should ask for copies of the policies and review them for regulatory compliance and ensure that they are updated. In highly regulated industries, the company may want the policies and procedures to be attached to the MSA. Companies will also want to be able to conduct periodic audits, either directly or using a third party, to review the provider's compliance with applicable law and the agreed-to policies and procedures. Strong remedies for failure to comply and for liabilities stemming from the provider's non-compliance are essential.

Providers to the financial services, health care, education, and other regulated industries are especially sensitive to these privacy and data security trends. Clients are asking more questions about their providers' security measures and regulatory compliance, especially where consumer data is involved. As a result, providers are having to increase budgets for data security technology and management to satisfy client demands and to comply with regulations. As service providers are gaining more awareness of the risk exposure and potential liability associated with these issues, they are becoming more resistant to risk-shifting provisions that place more liability on them for data breaches. More service providers are seeking to cap their liability for critical issues that have traditionally been excluded from contractual liability caps, such as security breach issues. This is not surprising, given that many reported security breaches are now costing companies millions of dollars per incident to remedy.

At the same, time, clients are becoming more knowledgeable about privacy and security laws and increasing their scrutiny of outsource providers and their security measures. Clients are requesting greater representations and warranties around these areas, tightening service level agreements (SLAs) that involve performance issues related to regulatory risk, and asking for more of the risk to shift to providers in the event of a security breach. On the liability issues, clients are also becoming more sensitive to providers that try to cap their liability for claims arising from security breaches. Clients are having to assess their total exposure and consider the likelihood of a doomsday scenario in some cases in deciding whether to cap the provider's liability or in deciding on the maximum liability that they will agree to.

Attorney Role in Managing Risk

The attorney needs to be involved in the early stages of the outsourcing process—preferably at the strategic planning phase—to guide the company in properly assessing the legal risks with the outsourcing decision and selecting the outsourcing provider. An attorney experienced in outsourcing can advise on what is market, the hot-button issues that will be encountered in negotiations, regulatory issues that may affect who is selected, and the overall structure of the transaction, including proper assessment of service levels and credits. It is best if the attorney can be consulted in drafting the RFP so that key legal issues can be addressed during the selection and due diligence phases where some of these issues could ideally be addressed with each candidate.

Attorneys can also guide companies in thinking about how to address these risks through the master services agreement, a properly drafted scope of work, and if applicable, through service level agreements. It is not just the property representations and warranties, indemnification, termination provisions, and other remedies that lawyers traditionally help with, but also the service level structure, the service level credits, and how to structure the agreement to incentivize the provider to perform in a way that is beneficial for both parties. The attorney can also help by drafting the statement of work to make the scope, as well as the process of how to address scope changes, very clear. Experienced outsourcing attorneys understand that most issues in outsourcing contracts revolve around disagreements about whether a task is in scope or out of scope. Many of these issues can be avoided by specific scope of work descriptions and clearly defined change order processes.

Careful drafting of the agreement will also help reduce the risks of other types of common issues. Attorneys are able to look for inconsistencies and errors in the documents, which becomes especially important as the documents become more complex. For example, an outsourcing deal may include a master services agreement, a statement of work, a service level agreement, a license agreement, and a maintenance services agreement, which all must work together. Making sure that all documents work together and do not contradict each other is important because inconsistencies lead to disputes. For example, sometimes documents will come to the attorney that contain separate limitations of liability in the MSA and in the SLA, perhaps related to different tasks or product offerings. The attorney can sort through these provisions to make sure they all are consistent and interact properly.

Components of Outsourcing Deals

Scope of Services

The scope of services that will be provided must be understood up front, to assess the risks involved. The type and volume of services being provided will affect the specific service levels that will be of concern. Cloud-based services that require constant availability and performance over time will affect the service levels differently than services based on transactions or milestones. It is important to ask the right questions of the service provider when discussing their expected performance. For example, how will they staff the services? Where will the services be performed? What quality control will they have in place? How will they address defects and performance errors? Will they need to subcontract any of the functions? These types of questions will help the company assess the risks connected with the services being provided. Companies also need to know that the scope of services is the biggest area of dispute in outsourcing contracts. The more detailed the contract, the less likely it is that a dispute will arise. Sometimes, companies will try to save time up front and not address the hard issues on certain service details by adding general descriptions of the service in the scope of work and adding language that the parties will mutually agree on the details at a later time. A "wait and see" approach to the service details could be costly and result in disputes. Key leverage could be lost once the parties are deeper into the relationship.

Service Levels

Service levels measure how well the provider is performing the services described in the agreement and provide a remedy for performance failures. Service levels should focus on critical risks and not every aspect of the services. The service levels need to be measurable and manageable, meaning there has to be objective criteria that can be met and there must be sufficient data for both parties to be able to determine if the service level has been obtained. Sometimes—especially where companies are outsourcing these services for the first time—they may not have sufficient data to understand where to set the targets. If companies are performing the same services in-house, hopefully, they are measuring their own performance. If they are not, they should start once the strategic decision to outsource is determined so that they have sufficient data to set the performance targets. In some industries, commonly provided services will have customary performance targets. If possible, companies should think through and list their service level objectives in the RFP process and solicit each prospect's proposed service level it is willing to agree to. Some outsourcing contracts may need to employ a ramp-up period in which the parties begin their relationship and collect data to set the appropriate service level. In these situations, it is very important to set out a clear process for how the service levels will be selected.

Sometimes—especially in business process outsourcing—a client will identify a large list of critical parts of the service and will want to try to measure and assess the risk of every aspect of each part. An SLA with a large number of different performance targets will become unmanageable and will not deliver value. Companies should focus only on the most critical items that will affect their business goals that can be measured objectively, and that both parties can monitor. Companies need to remember that objectives are worthless unless they can be both measured and monitored and the company has the resources to do so. Companies need to make sure that the amount of time required in monitoring the service is not going to be more time-consuming than performing the service itself. Companies also need to understand that not all service levels have the same degree of associated risk. It may be best in certain circumstances to quantify the risk associated with different parts of the services and assign different values to them for calculating any service credits due for performance failures. In some situations, the various service levels may not work in harmony and will have to be balanced accordingly. For example, one service level may focus on the speed of performing a task, but another may focus on quality. Depending on the way the service levels are weighted, the provider may sacrifice quality over speed, which would not achieve the company's desired goal.

The company should ensure that the provider has a quality assurance process in place to support the SLA. The company should require total transparency in the quality assurance process. The company also needs to ensure that it receives periodic reports that detail the service levels and provides the specific data on which the service level was calculated, including supportive background documentation.

Pricing and KPIs

Pricing can vary by service and by industry. Companies like to have consistent, predictable costs, and so fixed pricing is often sought. Providers prefer to pass through costs to their clients on a time-and-materials basis, to lessen their risk of having to perform at a loss. There are variations of both of these in different outsourcing relationships where some portions are fixed, while others that are perhaps more labor-intensive and unpredictable will be priced on a cost-plus basis to pass through labor costs at a mark-up of a certain percentage of cost. These affect the service level credits because the pricing model will affect how the parties calculate the credits for service failures. Sometimes, providers will want to include key performance indicators (KPIs) in the pricing model with performance goals that could increase the price for superior performance by the provider, or that can be used to offset service level credits for failed performance. Conversely, the service levels themselves will also affect the pricing because if the company requires a high level of performance, the provider may charge a higher price because of the perceived risk or the additional resources it must employ to achieve the desired level of service. Companies need to be careful that providers do not try to include KPIs that reward the provider for performing at the expected level, instead including KPIs that truly reward providers for performing beyond expectations.

Service Level Terms and Conditions

The SLA terms need to fit within the overall contract terms and conditions, and both need to be consistent with the other. Service level failure can affect provisions dealing with limitations of liability, indemnification, representations and warranties, *force majeure* scenarios, termination, and various covenants. The company should consider what level of failure of performance would cause it to exercise significant remedies and whether at some point, service level credits may be insufficient. Companies should be careful to ensure that service level credits do not negate other available remedies for significant performance issues. Additionally, defined terms that affect service level performance standards or that are used in calculating service levels need to be carefully drafted. For example, in cloud-based agreements, some commonly used terms like "uptime," "downtime," and "availability," can be too vague and make it difficult to identify when the performance level has been breached, especially when there is no time frame identifying when this performance will be measured. In other types of service level agreements, there may be broad terms that provide that the target performance will be measured based on a "successful" transaction, or it will provide that a certain result must be "achieved." These types of terms need to be clearly defined. Many times these types of terms are used without thinking through the scenarios in which a default could occur and the difficulty in properly identifying whether a remedy will be available if terms are to loosely worded. Companies should ensure that terms clearly identify at what point in time the measure of failure will be objectively observed. Another common item to watch out for is placing "reasonable efforts" or "commercially reasonable efforts" language in front of the service level to be achieved to dilute the service level's effectiveness. Lawyers should help their clients think through the scenarios so that there is no room for future dispute.

Another area to be careful of is that Providers are becoming less risk averse and are attempting to insert broad clauses into their contracts that absolve them from liability and excuse performance (including from the giving of service level credits) for a variety of causes in addition to the typical *force majeure*-type events. There are many variations of these types of broad "excused performance" clauses. For example, providers may try to excuse performance for the company's information or instructions it provided to the service provider, or where the company has been negligent. Usually, these are drafted in a broad way to potentially affect all kinds of breaches for which the service provider would ordinarily not be excused from liability. Companies should resist these, try to narrow them, or exclude certain types of important liabilities from these provisions, such as for security breaches or breaches of confidentiality obligations.

Performance and Liability

One area of importance in detailing SLAs is to look carefully at the calculations and how the provider will achieve the performance target. If KPIs are used, then the interaction between credits and KPIs needs to be reviewed very carefully to ensure that failure to hit an SLA target in one area is not outweighed by meeting a KPI performance objective in another area, where the overall result is a failure to achieve the company's goals. Sometimes, the provider will try to structure the service level so that certain targets that are easier to obtain have a greater weight in determining whether credits are available. Service level credit and KPI calculations can be complex. Companies should consider adding sweeping clauses that provide that—notwithstanding certain KPIs being achieved— if certain key failures still occur, that the provider will be liable and no KPI credits will be earned.

Companies also need to be careful of service level credit caps on liability. These interact with the standard limitations of liability in the MSA and must not be overlooked. Companies should try to make clear that service level caps are for performance failures that act as a price adjustment, not as damages. Service level credits should be viewed as a way to achieve goals, not necessarily to penalize the provider for substandard performance. The proper use of credits and/or KPIs can be beneficial for both parties. Providers will sometimes try to treat service level credits as the exclusive remedy for breaches and may argue that the service level credits will be used to reduce the overall damages cap in the MSA, like a vanishing deductible. Companies need to be careful that the contract wording is clear that the credits are not the only remedy and do not reduce any damages or caps on liability available to the company for the provider's breach. Variations of this concept can be negotiated, but it is something that needs to be carefully reviewed.

Technical Considerations

Companies should consider to what extent technology affects the performance of the outsourcing provider. Sometimes, the company may require the provider to use the company's software, equipment, or other systems so that it has more control over performance issues. The company may need to license software to the provider and be responsible for updating and maintaining the software for the provider's use. Any technology provided by the company or by the provider needs to be considered in determining whether a service level is not achieved.

Managing the Outsourcing Relationship

Managing the outsourcing relationship after the contract is signed is very important to success. One of the biggest areas where disputes arise in contracts is in the process of changing the scope of work. These disputes can often arise when communication breaks down and the provider changes the scope without obtaining proper client approval, or the client needs a change to the services to address a concern, such as a change in regulatory requirements. Making sure there is a clear path for each party to request, review, and approve changes prior to implementation will reduce the risks of a dispute over these types of issues. Sometimes, it may be best to have a different change order process for regulatory issues and a different level and timing of approval, such as requiring the change be approved unless it would cause substantial harm to the other party. Changes will often necessitate price adjustments, service level modifications, and changes to the service level credits. All of these could take time to negotiate. Companies should make sure that no changes can be implemented until the parties agree in writing or—if the arrangement needs more flexibility—that another process is implemented for minor changes. Companies must, however, clearly define what a minor change includes, while still requiring more important changes to be reflected in a signed change order or amendment.

To properly manage the communications between the parties, address concerns, and possibly head issues off before they erupt into disputes, the parties need to have a management structure in place. Companies should include provisions in the MSA that designate personnel responsible for communicating issues and resolving disputes. The parties should agree to regular meetings so that there is constant communication and interaction in which performance can be reviewed and objectives identified to address concerns. Especially in the beginning of the outsourcing contract term, the parties need to develop the relationship and work out the bugs. The management personnel assigned the contract may want to meet more frequently during the first year of the contract to ensure a smoother ramp up and transition. Depending on the complexity of the services being performed, the parties may wish to form a committee that will meet and decide these issues. The management structure should also include periodic reporting and the ability of the company to audit the provider's performance or regulatory compliance.

Relevant Statutes

Gramm-Leach Bliley Act (GLBA), Fair Credit Reporting Act (FCRA), the Health Insurance Portability and Accountability Act (HIPAA), the Health Information Technology for Economic and Clinical Health Act (HITECH), Family Educational Rights and Privacy Act (FERPA), California Financial Information Privacy Act (CFIPA), Foreign Corrupt Practice Act (FCPA), and related guidelines, rules and regulations, and state law equivalents.

Conclusion

Lawyers can play a key role in managing the risks of the outsourcing relationship for their clients. In the case where a client may be outsourcing a service for the first time, the lawyer needs to provide guidance at the early stages by alerting the client to major issues to watch out for. Even for experienced clients, outsourcing is often a financial decision and the lawyer needs to help the client think about the risks in the cost-benefit analysis. The earlier the lawyer can advise the client on its outsourcing strategy before the contract stage, the better. The lawyer can also be a valuable member of the team while negotiating the business issues surrounding the SLA. Since the SLA affects liability issues, breach, and remedies, the structuring of the SLA should be handled with the lawyer's full involvement. Lastly, the lawyer can help an outsourcing client to establish a clear management and approval process that can help avoid disputes and resolve them quickly when they do occur.

Key Takeaways

- Focus as much time and attention on the scope of work and on the change order process as spent on drafting and negotiating the MSA because this is where most disputes begin.

- If possible, companies should think through and list their service level objectives in the RFP process and solicit each prospect's proposed service level it is willing to agree to.

- Companies should focus only on the most critical service level items that will affect their business goals, that can be measured objectively, and that both parties can monitor.

- The company should ensure that the provider has a quality assurance process in place to support the SLA. The company should require total transparency in the quality assurance process.

- If KPIs are used, then the interaction between credits and KPIs needs to be reviewed very carefully to ensure that failure to hit an SLA target in one area is not outweighed by meeting a KPI performance objective in another area, where the overall result is a failure to achieve the company's goals.

Michael Orlando is a partner in the Del Mar Heights/San Diego, California office of Sheppard Mullin Richter & Hampton LLP, where he is a member of the Technology Transactions Team. He represents clients ranging from Fortune 500 companies to early-stage start-ups on a wide variety of complex technology and outsourcing transactions in multiple industries, including financial services, education, health care, life sciences, hardware, software, media, aerospace, sports equipment, apparel, and consumer products. He works with clients in developing their outsourcing strategies, negotiating and drafting outsourcing agreements, and assisting clients with issues that arise during the outsourcing relationship. His outsourcing experience includes outsourced manufacturing, development, information technology outsourcing (ITO), business process outsourcing (BPO), offshoring arrangements, strategic alliances, and joint ventures. Mr. Orlando received both a JD and an MBA from the University of San Diego, and a BA from the University of California, San Diego.

Dedication: *This chapter is dedicated to my wife Kim, and our three daughters Kayla, Malia, and Sophia for their love, support, patience, and tolerance.*

Outsourcing Governance and Program Management: An Evolution

Randall S. Parks

Chair, Global Technology and Outsourcing Practice Group
Hunton & Williams LLP

ASPATORE

Introduction

The outsourcing environment has changed significantly over the past ten years. Ten years ago, the mega-deal was still common. Multiple business functions were bundled into long-term agreements with single providers with total contract values in the billions of dollars. While those transactions still exist, they are far rarer now. Big deals mean the potential for big results, but they also mean big risks. Our industry has had its share of difficulties with these mega-deals, many of which did not survive, but it has evolved responses to those failures. Transactions are now much smaller. Risks are managed through diversification of suppliers, shorter contract terms, and better provider and program governance processes.

We have participated in this evolution and observed the performance difference that good governance can make. Signing a long-term outsourcing agreement is not the end of anything—it is just the beginning of the next phase of a continuous negotiation. Good governance processes structure that conversation. They fill gaps, manage change, overcome problems, drive new value, and preserve profitability. They convert a static agreement and economic model into a dynamic, vital relationship with the ability to persist and overcome challenges.

Key Elements of the Role of Governance in Today's Outsourcing Environment

In our experience, governance goes well beyond the scope of the governance schedule to a contract and the usual line-up of committees. We think some of the keys to good governance include:

Careful Provider Selection. There is a bell curve in everything, including outsourcing. Some providers are simply better than others are. Finding the better ones requires thorough investigation of capabilities. It can be easy to short-cut this process when the provider pool consists of the usual global players, assuming that size and longevity ensure quality. But size alone only ensures that both ends of the bell curve will be faithfully represented in the organization and longevity in a sector often is an illusion, as providers rapidly build, reconfigure, and shed businesses to respond to competition and changing priorities. Within firms, performance varies widely across business units, delivery teams, and account leadership.

Sifting the pool requires up-to-the-minute industry knowledge and critical reference checking. To avoid the tendency of references to understate failures, we suggest triangulating on the truth by obtaining more than one perspective from each reference. We suggest requiring providers to furnish references from relationships that have terminated early, as well those that have been successful. That has become routine and is largely accepted—but you have to be critical about what you are hearing. I have been surprised to hear a glowing reference come back from a customer that I knew had suffered mightily at the hands of the provider. Check the providers' litigation records for an inside view of problem transactions.

We also suggest that you interview the proposed delivery executives and be selective about who will join your team. You need not accept the provider's first offer. Once the roster is complete, insist that the team leaders be an active part of negotiations, so that they are as familiar as your own team with the guardrails in the contract and the reasons for them. Then keep that A-team on your account as long as you can—and as long as they continue to be the A-team.

Provider Diversification. Careful selection processes are bolstered by resilient multi-provider networks. Where a single provider concentrates risk and exposes the customer to a monopoly provider, two or more providers in a champion-challenger or jump-ball structure lowers the risk of failure and inspires healthy competition. We have seen the benefits of this strategy most clearly in the applications maintenance and development function, where several of our clients have contracted providers to bid for projects and share volume. The providers are (relatively) happy because each of them has won a piece of the opportunity. The customer is happy because it has avoided single vendor lock-in and has access to the deeper bench offered by multiple providers, all of whom are vying for the next project. Of course, some functions—such as IT infrastructure—cannot easily be divided and more providers means more governance resources, but where it can be done we find that the benefits far outweigh the costs.

Customer Alignment from the Top. Senior management and the key clients of the outsourced function need to understand the context for each relationship—its goals and limitations, what risks each party has assumed, where the deal is most likely to fail, and how those failures can be mitigated.

This can be a significant effort and requires advance planning and diligent execution. The one person you did not reach will be the one who submarines the relationship after contract execution.

Less obviously, alignment requires long-term maintenance, too. Periodic relationship reviews with the clients are important to remind the team of the original objectives, evaluate success, and initiate course corrections. Not keeping the team aligned risks letting relationship-destroying (and career-limiting) gaps grow between expectations and results.

Information technology leadership teams also change rapidly. The average CIO tenure is four or five years, whereas the average outsourcing agreement runs for three to five years. Given the odds that an outsourcing agreement will outlive its leadership, contract managers need to prepare to re-align succeeding generations of leaders. Where routine governance processes are in place, the business case and supporting data necessary to make that happen should be readily available.

Resilient Commercial Structures. Successful transactions are generally built on commercial structures that are easily understood and that respect the financial interests of both parties. Overly complex structures and obscure allocations of risk suggest the possibility of gamesmanship (real or imagined) and undermine trust. Structures that ruthlessly allocate gains to one side or the other tend to discourage those gains. Too much financial engineering (for example, by spreading implementation costs over a longer term than would ordinarily be agreed upon) creates an unhealthy lock-in, trading future flexibility for short-term gain. The immediate win is often forgotten years later when a massive early termination charge stands in the way of a new initiative. Likewise, provider insistence on termination charges not directly linked to any economic investment creates adversarial relationships where the parties ought to be collaborating to address new challenges.

We find the most successful commercial structures to be those that link performance to pay and customer success. The obvious examples are customer contact center transactions where the provider is paid only if it converts a sale. Providers have picked up on the natural attraction for customers of this approach and are offering "outcome based" pricing models for an expanding range of transactional business processes. Some providers claim that 80 percent or more of their contracts now have an outcome-based component. When these deals properly align the provider's performance with the customer's business objectives, they become more self-governing. The providers tend to like these models because they allow them to escape the relentless commoditization of pricing models that are simply cost-plus arrangements. Instead, they feel they can focus more intensely on delivering value to the customer—while at the same time preserving their ability take cost out of their own processes without necessarily having to share the gain with their customers. Customers may be happy with this new alignment and the focus on value, but should take the same precautions to maintain competition as they might have in more traditional structures.

Though intermittently out of favor with the consultancies, we continue to think that benchmarking is a useful tool to inspire conversations about whether value is actually being delivered and to rebalance otherwise frozen economics. Some consultants have very publicly denied the value of benchmarking and a minority of providers resist it. Those providers claim to believe that fair and accurate benchmarking is an illusion and that they cannot possibly subject their already-narrow profit margins to the black-box methodology of a consultant whose success depends on proving that every deal he sees is overpriced. Yet those very same providers are contributors and subscribers to the databases used by those consultants. They use them to price check their offerings. That same minority are active saboteurs, attempting to defang the contractual provisions at the outset and then subverting the process in operation by strong-arming the consultants and delaying the process. Fortunately, many providers more understand that a strong benchmarking clause can be a relationship enhancer that builds client confidence in longer-term deals. We have often seen a strong benchmarking clause be part of the trade for an extended term.

To be useful, a benchmarking clause needs to be balanced and produce a credible, certain outcome. A benchmarking process that calls only for a conversation and does not result in an automatic adjustment of out-of-bounds pricing is toothless and a waste of time. Likewise, a process that demands that the provider meet the best price—however low—offered by every player attempting to buy market share will not result in a sustainable deal. We have found success with a benchmarking approach that requires a mandatory price adjustment based on the mid-point (or even the upper quartile) of the competition, but that also ignores small price deviations and stop-losses the adjustment for the provider if there is a major dislocation. Importantly, we put the benchmark entirely in the hands of a pre-agreed slate of consultants and eliminate the opportunity for either side to frustrate the process by challenging each decision along the way. There is plenty of opportunity for discussion, but the consultant's methodology governs and its professional judgment is final. A sample benchmarking clause reflecting these ideas appears in Appendix A.

The evolution of data-driven "virtual benchmarking" techniques has made the process an even more useful tool. Consultancies such as Alsbridge/ProBenchmark use deep databases, in many cases supplemented by the vendors themselves, to produce quick, economical price comparisons. Where a traditional benchmark might take three months and $250,000 in fees, virtual benchmarking can be done in a couple of weeks for a fraction of the cost. We have used them to validate pricing and inject some competitive tension into sole source procurements where other factors precluded a multi-party competition.

Govern Yourself! Oddly enough, you should be careful not to negotiate too hard. Providers in competitive situations are more likely to oversell their capacities and take on more risk than is prudent. When this happens, the relationship is doomed. Provider investment vanishes under the press to cut costs, and your carefully recruited A-team starts looking for a more promising vehicle to advance their careers. Unless the customer is willing to bail out the provider, an early, acrimonious termination soon follows. That is bad enough, but these disasters often poison the organization entirely against outsourcing as a useful business tool, cutting it off from all of the benefits of the practice. While sometimes difficult to achieve under tight budgets and a bit unusual, we often discuss allowing a contingency fund to offset provider financial missteps. Spreading a bit of extra cash to the provider in a pinch can avoid a much greater loss from unwinding the deal.

Use the Contract to Your Benefit. Too many times during a negotiation someone laughingly says, "If we ever have to pull this contract out of the drawer, we will all be in trouble!" When I hear that, I know trouble has already arrived. Usually, the speaker is a successful old hand in the department who has seen it all and has great confidence in their ability to negotiate a fix to any situation. In the past, they have usually relied on their ability to manage employees or their leverage as a big customer. In a significant outsourcing deal, however, both of those advantages are little to no help. The customer is locked into a long-term agreement, which diminishes leverage and is the only direct means of influencing the provider's behavior. Worse, the provider teams are almost certainly far better trained at using the agreement to their advantage (they do it for a living) and resisting attempts to apply pressure outside the contract. At best, the provider will be better able to insist on strict adherence to the deal that was cut. At worst, the account team will exploit the vulnerabilities of the arrangement and their superior tactical knowledge of its terms to maximize their outcomes to the customer's detriment. We have seen it happen again and again—notwithstanding all the warm assurances of partnership and trust exchanged at the signing table.

Because of that, we try to adjust the thinking of the old hand as soon as possible. There is no doubt that outsourcing agreements can be long and tedious documents. However, they represent the rules of physics for the deal and cannot be ignored any more than gravity. Getting the right rules clearly established and then knowing how to work with them is critical to success. We find that customers routinely under-invest in the contract management skills of their retained teams—both in terms of headcount and substantive training. For many years, we have been advising our clients to select the management team carefully and train them thoroughly. We will often go back several months into the implementation to review the contract with the team again. They always have far more—and much more educated—questions after having lived with it.

In addition to the self-aligning commercial structures mentioned earlier, some of the basic contract terms that we have found to be crucial governance tools are:

<u>Focused, Flexible Service Levels.</u> Service levels (and credits for failing to meet them) are essential to focus both parties on defining and meeting business-oriented performance targets. When well done, they provide an objective measure of success and a basis for delivering increasing value.

When constructed by rote, they are a distraction, a source of friction, and a waste of effort—leading to the ironic industry complaint "My service levels are green, but why do I see red?" The industry has become much better at editing the service levels for many functions and more closely aligning them with the customer's underlying business goals. The best teams build service levels that naturally align provider behavior with the customer's ultimate goals. When coupled with outcome-based pricing models, these transactions deliver real value in ways that are immediately obvious.

We also routinely require flexibility in the service level model to allow for changing business priorities and processes. Our models, which are common in the industry, allow the customer to add, drop, and change service levels and credit allocations periodically. Providers reasonably ask for some limitations on this flexibility to protect the basic financial assumptions of their profit model, but understand that it builds customer confidence in the resilience of the partnership. Oddly, we find that this tool is often overlooked and underused by customer teams, particularly the provisions for establishing new service levels.

Key Personnel. Because success depends so much on the skills and accumulated knowledge of the provider team, we recommend that our clients reserve significant control over it. The ability to select the key players and to remove them at will is critical. Often the most direct and immediate means of affecting provider behavior is to require removal of an under-performing on-site delivery manager, and we have seen dramatic turnarounds following a change. Of course, abusing that power has the same negative effects on contractors that it would have on employees. Having outsourced the function, many customers have little patience with performance issues on provider teams and rapidly develop a hypercritical we/they mentality. Customer leadership should be on guard for this phenomenon and temper it appropriately. While you are paying a premium for, and should demand, competent management, your success depends too much on the provider personnel to discard them without a real attempt to build that competency where you can.

Once you have achieved that competency, you should insist that the key individuals stay on your account for a reasonable period of time—usually at least two years plus any particularly difficult periods, such as a major platform transition. Some providers whose local markets have high turnover will resist this, arguing that it will discourage the best talent from joining the team. If the best talent wants to reserve the right to abandon the team quickly, then we question whether we truly want them on board. Most providers will agree to reasonable restrictions on turnover.

<u>Complete Performance; No Abandonment.</u> One of the key "rules of physics" on which we insist is provider agreement to full performance of its contracted obligations. While that may seem obvious, provider legal teams routinely salt their mark-ups with qualifying language, such as "...provider will perform the Services *in all material respects* as described in the Statement of Work..." Our joking response is that we will accept that if they agree that the customer can pay the provider's bill "in all material respects." No one has made that trade yet. The point is the same—the parties should expect each other to do 100 percent of what is agreed.

However, the common law is not entirely on our side here, allowing behaviors such as "substantial performance" and "efficient breach"— both of which permit less than the 100 percent performance on which our clients' success depends. As a result, we back up the service descriptions with an express agreement not to refuse to perform or abandon any part of the services and a right to a quick injunction if that promise is broken. Unfortunately, some providers have as much as told us that they know they cannot deliver more than 90–95 percent of the services, and that they fully expect to simply drop small parts that are uneconomical for them to deliver. Without the "no abandonment" clause, the customer has little practical remedy—termination hurts more than it helps, and a lawsuit cannot recover lost revenues and profits from nonperformance, since those are typically waived. When we encounter resistance to this clause, we know we have found one of those providers and push all the harder to include it.

Deploy Thoughtful Governance Structures. Good contract terms are supported with a thoughtfully designed governance structure. At the deal level, we find that the classic three-level structure works well—line management handles daily issues, departmental management addresses tactical direction and first-level disputes, and executive management deals with strategy and more serious unresolved problems. The keys to the most successful structures include:

<u>Well-Defined Roles On Both Sides</u>. When performance is divided between parties, knowing exactly who has the ball at any point in time is critical to avoiding the usual finger-pointing when the ball drops. That implies investing substantial effort in drafting the statements of work to be attached to the agreement. There are practical limitations on how much you can write down and how much the parties are willing to invest in the process. However, ambiguity and omission are rarely the customer's friend. The customers' business success depends on full performance and the provider has a tremendous negotiating advantage when saying "no" means that new revenues or cost savings are delayed. Accordingly, we prepare our clients for a long slog in building the statements of work and insist on fair contractual provisions that keep the provider working during any dispute over scope.

<u>Skilled Transaction Managers On Both Sides</u>. This is easy to say and much harder to execute. Routinely, we find that problem deals suffer from management gaps. On the customer side, the excellent operational managers who managed the outsourced function do not automatically become excellent contract managers. Avoiding the "old hand" problem mentioned above requires some forward thinking by more senior management. The skills necessary to manage a provider through a complex agreement are not the same required to manage employees, and a front-end investment in vendor management training will pay off over the life of the deal. The evolution of the industry toward multiple smaller transactions has exacerbated this vulnerability. Smaller deals have resulted in more customer-managed multi-provider ecosystems, which require the skills to integrate the transactions, mediate between the providers, and realize efficiencies from enforcing uniformity of vocabulary and practice. These "program management" skills are in increasing demand, and it is no coincidence that the sourcing consultancies have developed robust products, some supported by elaborate software tools, to help fill the gaps in customer skill sets.

On the provider side, common customer complaints include a sudden shift from enthusiastic sales mode to green eyeshade hyper-focus on account profitability, which drains flexibility from the arrangement and makes innovation (at least, the sort that delivers value to the customer) difficult to produce. This behavior is very difficult to manage. When it occurs, we find that there has usually been an error in provider selection or in constructing the economics of the deal. The more typical kinds of underperformance can be dealt with by changing the team, as described above.

Relentless Governance. Transactions and providers will not manage themselves. Establishing the routines of governance—reports, meetings, and agendas—and relentlessly sticking to them is essential discipline. They provide the forum for addressing failures and change and for celebrating successes. Where those routines fall apart during periods of calm, we find that they are very difficult to resuscitate when a problem develops. Instead of the comfort of routine, those reconstituted meetings have an air of desperation and failure that overshadows the recovery effort.

Frank, Early Engagement Of Failure. Too often when there is a failure, customers are reluctant to engage the formal performance management tools available under the contract because they feel that they will result in a hostile escalation. That will certainly be true if you use them only when you mean to be hostile. However, when well-designed and engaged routinely within the boundaries of established governance cadences, they lose their edge and become the tool for professional engagement of problem issues that they were intended to be. A breach notice sent once a year on your lawyer's letterhead is very different from one delivered at a weekly meeting as a problem first begins to emerge. Importantly, these notices provide the documentary foundation that is necessary to enforce your rights if it should come to that. If you do not create a paper trail, the contract will become far less useful and you will have devalued your options. Just as importantly, delaying frank engagement creates the opportunity for surprisingly effective "moral" arguments that would not be out of place on the playground: "You did not tell me it was a problem" or "I thought it was okay because you did not say anything." Hitting a little closer to home—if you do not do these things early on, your management will be right in asking why you did not.

Embracing Change. Renegotiations are common and often happen early. They are an inevitable part of the lifecycle of complex relationships. No matter how much effort is involved in the planning and negotiation of the deal, the structure must often be modified to reflect the actual problems of execution. Preparing the customer team—including management—for this eventuality is an important part of the program management team's responsibility. The customer leader for one of our most resilient IT transactions has implemented an annual renegotiation process, which has been important for the longevity of that relationship with a very difficult provider.

Trust? Recently, the industry has heard from many that "trust" is the key to successful outsourcing relationships. However, trust cannot come first. Handing a key function to a third party based in any significant part on trust would just be reckless. Investors and boards of directors have been burned far too many times to do business based on trust. The outsourcing practitioner who says that "trust" is the basis for next year's forecast can prepare for a pay cut—if not a new job.

That is not to say that there is not a role for trust in outsourcing. Every business partnership is an act of faith—faith that the other person can and will deliver on their promises. That trust is earned, in part, through repeated delivery against commitments. That is the sort of trust that forms the basis for the measured risk-taking that produces outsize returns. It is also the sort of trust that builds through good governance, which encourages, measures, and celebrates the repeated wins it needs to grow.

Conclusion

Many lawyers think of vendor management and governance as the sole province of the management consultants – just so many PowerPoint slides with flow charts and lists of "two in a box" provider/customer personnel pairings. Smart sourcing lawyers know otherwise. If only to protect the integrity of their beautifully drafted and artfully negotiated agreement, sourcing lawyers have to understand the importance of ensuring that those who will manage it understand why it works the way it does and how to pull its levers. Getting that message across requires good lawyering, but also leadership and change management skills that many clients do not look for in their outside counsel. As multi-provider environments proliferate and the pace of change among providers and their service offerings continues to accelerate, demand for that skill set will only increase. Sourcing lawyers are in an ideal position to meet that demand and help their clients—and often their consultants—get it right.

Key Takeaways

- Governance means you. Be an active part of your client's outsourcing governance discussions. You are the architect of the contractual "rules of physics" that will bind the new relationship and an essential educator, interpreter and advisor.

- Governance extends well beyond the contract. Help your client weed out the dangerous providers early. Consider multi-provider structures to reduce failure risk.

- Do not assume alignment throughout the customer. Senior management and the key clients of the outsourced function need to understand the context for each relationship—its goals and limitations, what risks each party has assumed, where the deal is most likely to fail, and how those failures can be mitigated. Periodic relationship reviews are important to remind the team of the original objectives, evaluate success, and initiate course corrections.

- Build resilient commercial structures that naturally align interests, such as "pay for performance" or "outcome-based" pricing. Understand that a strong benchmarking clause can be a relationship enhancer that builds client confidence in longer-term deals. To be useful, a benchmarking clause needs to be balanced and produce a credible, certain outcome.

- Build service levels that naturally align provider behavior with the customer's ultimate goals. When coupled with outcome-based pricing models, these transactions deliver real value in ways that are immediately obvious. Require flexibility in the service level model to allow for changing business priorities and processes

- Govern aggressively and relentlessly. Outsourcing requires continuous maintenance to succeed. Build the tools to get it done and use them to monitor the deal and intervene early.

Randall S. Parks is chair of Hunton & Williams LLP's Global Technology and Outsourcing Practice Group, co-chair of its Retail Industry Practice Group and serves on the firm's Executive Committee. His practice focuses on complex commercial transactions, particularly business process and information technology outsourcing, e-commerce, licensing, systems acquisition, development and integration agreements, manufacturing, supply, distribution, and complex services agreements and multi-country joint ventures. During his career, he has negotiated and documented dozens of large-scale, complex global transactions worth billions of dollars. Mr. Parks' experience also includes public and private securities offerings and corporate disclosure under the 1933 and 1934 Acts, corporate governance, and mergers and acquisitions and a broad range of corporate counseling. He has been named *among the leading outsourcing lawyers in* Chambers USA *and* Legal 500 United States *and has consistently been recognized in* The Best Lawyers in America *for information technology, corporate law, and mergers and acquisitions.*

Creating and Maintaining a Successful Relationship with Outsourcing Vendors

Monica Verma

Partner

Baker & Hostetler LLP

ASPATORE

Introduction

Outsourcing, when performed well, can result in a company receiving cost savings and increased efficiency. But like any long-term relationship, making it last is the real challenge. Most companies fall into the trap of thinking that the entire outsourcing process is complete after the contract is executed by the parties. However, signing the contract is only the start of the business relationship and management of an outsourcing relationship is essential to ensure long-term success. It is important to conduct initial due diligence on vendors to choose the right party that will be a good cultural fit with the company and understands the values that are important to the company. As both parties to the outsourcing relationship will have their own social and cultural differences, these differences have to be recognized and bridged throughout the term of the relationship.

Reasons to Outsource and Trends

Cost reduction remains one of the main reasons to outsource, and is still used as the primary reason during presentations of business cases for outsourcing to executives. In addition to cost savings, another reason for outsourcing is increasing quality. Outsourcing often leads to better access to talented and skilled resources that are available on demand and can assist with meeting changing market conditions and improving business performance. Companies that are looking for low-cost multilingual work force are seeking "near shoring" opportunities in Tier 1 and Tier 2 cities located in Central America, Mexico, and Canada. In addition, due to the existence of free-trade zone, the Central American and Caribbean contact center outsourcing services markets are also gaining momentum.

Information technology (IT) remains a strong area for outsourcing. The expansion of business process outsourcing (BPO) continues in areas such as finance, accounting, procurement, and human resources (HR) and within these areas, still the most common functions that are outsourced are the ones that are considered non-core, such as data processing, IT, payroll, billing, and coding.

Key Internal Team for Outsourcing Relationship

A company that is considering outsourcing should have the right internal management team involved in the decision-making process. It is important to make sure that the appropriate decisions and approvals are obtained before embarking on the outsourcing journey. In many cases, certain departments move ahead in the decision-making process and then have to end up backtracking to get executive or board level approval.

It is also important that in addition to the management team and resources that provide area expertise for the function that is being outsourced, the outsourcing team should also consist of the following expertise: technical, HR, legal, and security. The inclusion of such experts early on will help avoid some of the complicated issues relating to compliance with laws and with the terms of third-party contracts.

Outsourcing oftentimes involves rebadging of current employees to the vendor and may involve decisions relating to internal reduction in force. Both the internal HR department and legal team can assist with the planning and compliance issues when any such decisions are made along with the outsourcing process. Across all sectors, companies are facing very sensitive issues with respect to access, use, and protection of personal data. In the case of multinational companies, the laws of different countries relating to the handling of personal data also add to the complexity in this area. The European Union (EU), for example, is looking to introduce new regulations regarding this issue, which means that the levels of fines and penalties for misuse of personal data will likely become significantly greater. On January 25, 2012, the European Commission proposed a comprehensive reform of the EU's 1995 data protection rules to strengthen online data protection rights. For purposes of compliance with privacy laws in different jurisdictions, it is becoming important to focus on where data will be stored and who will have access to it. By including the technical, security, and legal experts on the team will ensure protection of personal data and compliance with laws.

In addition, the issue relating to providing access to third-party software to vendors is prevalent in all industries and across all types of outsourcing. If access to third-party software is granted by a company to a vendor and such third-party agreements are not reviewed to see if such access is allowed, this could result in later claims of breach of contract and even infringement of intellectual property (IP) rights. Also, there may be issues with respect to receiving cooperation from third-party software providers if the vendor is considered a competitor of those software providers. It is advisable to review, with the assistance of legal team, the applicable third-party contracts when an internal decision to outsource is being made to evaluate any risks associated with granting such access to the vendor and any costs associated with increased fees resulting from such access.

Key Considerations in Creating and Managing the Outsourcing Relationship:

Selection of vendor: It is important to outline clear technical and business requirements in the request for proposal (RFP). By setting clear requirements, it will be easier to get more tailored responses from vendors. Also, state up front in the RFP that form responses will not be considered. Conducting background checks and due diligence on providers is also key. Companies should look into the provider's service delivery history, financial stability, and industry experience; conduct site visits; and meet with their management and delivery team. Obtaining the names of other customers is not enough; a company should call those customers and conduct reference checks. Read the feedback and reviews provided by other customers regarding the vendors.

It is essential to make sure that a strong vendor team is selected by the company based on a review of resumes and skill sets and meetings with the team members. The face-to-face meeting is an opportunity to get to know the team that will be providing the services. Since turnover in the outsourcing industry is high, it is essential that after the selection process, the selected vendor team is available for performance of continued services.

Definition of Requirements and Transition of Services: There is normally no such thing as a fixed-fee contract. If the vendor's requirements are not clearly defined and the statement of work (SOW) allows for later clarifications in scope and service levels, that situation may be cause for a price increase. There should be baselines and performance assumptions. If actual work exceeds the estimates and/or the assumptions are not accurate, then the customer is typically required to pay the difference. Most projects change by 10–15 percent during the development cycle. It is important to clearly define work-related expectations and any scope requirements in the SOW to avoid later issues with respect to pricing.

In addition, attention needs to be given to completion time and cost of knowledge transfers and to successful completion of transition services. These issues can be managed by building in contract provisions such as milestones and payments tied to milestones, penalties for delay, and the right to not move to the next stage. For instance, a company needs to consider how to transfer technical and business knowledge to a vendor—a process that normally requires a substantial time commitment and investment. A company typically thinks that most of its work is done when it executes the outsourcing agreement and the SOW. However, the actual heavy lifting starts during the transition period. It is important to keep the internal team motivated to continue supporting the vendor during the transition period, as this is a critical milestone for successful execution of the relationship. Some companies use various bonus structures and, in some cases, retention agreements for motivating their internal staff and to ensure continued support and availability of the internal staff for successful completion of the knowledge transfer and transition of the outsourced function.

Management of the Relationship: The management of the outsourcing relationship may be considered as an unnecessary overhead by a company but the fact is that an outsourcing company needs to invest in and focus on the continued management of the relationship with its vendor. Often, companies mistakenly believe that their work will automatically be done when the outsourcing contract is signed. In fact, the outsourcing relationship needs to be monitored and managed throughout the term. The company should know the team that will be providing its vendor services and these relationships need to be nurtured and developed by the company to create a long-term and successful outsourcing relationship. Managing remote teams is not easy and inadequate communication is one of the highest ranked causes for failure of outsourcing relationships. Regularly scheduled meetings, social events, and visits to the local service locations of the vendor to talk about successes and issues will help foster strong and long-term relationships. Personality clashes need to be recognized and resolved. Also, it is best to prevent confrontations and avoid a blame culture. If the person in charge of managing the relationship understands and is aware of the social and cultural differences of the vendor team and is able to bridge those gaps, such a person will be more successful in managing the relationship with the vendor team.

Termination Assistance and Knowledge Transfer: Not all outsourcing relationships last forever, despite the parties' best intentions and efforts. It is best to be prepared and to have a plan in place prior to any termination or expiration of the outsourcing agreement. In the event of the termination or expiration of the outsourcing agreement, the company needs to review the scope of the project and the time it will need to transition the services in-house or to a third-party vendor. The current vendor's resources will be required to transfer knowledge to the new vendor or the company's employees. Based on where the data was hosted, the current vendor may be required to transfer all data and work product. Each of the specific assistance requirements and the timeframe for such assistance and cooperation should be laid out in the contingency plan early in the relationship to avoid any future disputes and such plan should be updated periodically.

Conclusion

Successful outsourcing relationships can be structured and managed when each party explores their respective expectations, capabilities, and cultures, appreciates one another's goals and requirements, and understands what deficiencies must be overcome and what differences must be reconciled. These conversations, together with due diligence and regular management of the outsourcing relationship, will most likely reduce the likelihood of failure.

Key Takeaways

- Make sure that the appropriate decisions and approvals from the management team and board (if applicable) are obtained before embarking on the outsourcing journey. Ensure that in addition to the management team resources that provide area expertise for the function that is being outsourced, the outsourcing team should also consist of the following expertise: technical, HR, legal, and security.

- Keep in mind that companies that engage in outsourcing need to deal with various regulatory compliance issues relating to personal data. Focus on where data will be stored and who will have access to it.

- Review third-party contracts when an internal decision to outsource is being made to evaluate any risks associated with granting access to third-party software to the vendor, such as breach of contract and intellectual property infringement claims.

- Outline clear technical and business requirements in the request for proposal (RFP). Conducting background checks and due diligence on providers is key.

- Consider how to incentivize the internal team to assist with the knowledge transfer to a vendor—a process that normally requires a substantial time commitment and investment.

- Understand that the outsourcing relationship needs to be monitored, nurtured, and managed during the term of the agreement.

- Each of the specific termination assistance requirements and the timeframe for such assistance and cooperation should be laid out in the contingency plan early in the relationship to avoid any future disputes and such plan should be updated periodically.

Monica Verma, a partner with Baker & Hostetler LLP, has a diverse practice that includes outsourcing and technology transactions. Her experience, with respect to sourcing transactions, includes representing customers in information technology and business process outsourcing, as well as handling all aspects of such transactions, including management of the RFP process, drafting, and negotiations of outsourcing agreements. She has extensive experience working with Fortune 500 companies and mid cap companies, regularly counseling clients on how to address risks associated with implementation and integration, acceptance testing, system configuration, service level agreements, transition planning, and other common areas of exposure in technology contracting. She provides practical guidance to companies to identify transactional benefits and risks, assists companies in crafting strategies to address and overcome risks associated with technology and outsourcing agreements, and aids in closing deals within tight budgets and timetables.

Ms. Verma is also licensed to practice law in India. Because of her background, knowledge, and experience with India and its laws, she is able to help clients bridge cross-border differences in business and social culture, language, geopolitical risk, logistical infrastructure, and dispute resolution processes to achieve successful outcomes when dealing with cross-border transactions.

Cloud Computing, Multi-Sourcing Create New Challenges in Outsourcing

Michael J. Brito

Partner

Akin Gump Strauss Hauer & Feld LLP

ASPATORE

Introduction

There are two significant trends in outsourcing: the emergence of cloud computing, and the increased use of multiple-service providers in a customer's technology environment (multi-sourcing).

Cloud Computing

In the past twelve months, businesses have increasingly taken advantage of the benefits of using cloud-based services. In addition to technology, media, and public-sector clients, a number of other industry segments have embraced the cloud, including transportation and manufacturing.

As a general matter, enterprise cloud delivery models feature "on-demand" or readily scalable services and pricing is based on consumption. From a business or customer perspective, cloud-based solutions have lower costs, require no up-front capital investment, align the cost with consumption (paying only for amounts actually consumed), and shift the risk of obsolescence or upgrading technology to the cloud provider.

In an effort to take advantage of the increased appetite for cloud-based service, service providers have been actively seeking ways in which to enhance their cloud-based offerings. As a result, there has been significant increase in mergers and acquisitions (M&A) activity in the cloud space. For example, IBM recently acquired SoftLayer. Analysts believe that the deal will enable IBM to compete more aggressively for small- and medium-size businesses and offer a broader range of public cloud options to large enterprises. Service providers have also announced various strategic partnerships and alliances intended to enhance delivery capabilities.

With all of the economic benefits of an enterprise cloud solution, there are a number of limitations. As a general rule, legacy cloud providers are less flexible when negotiating the terms and conditions that govern the cloud solution. In general, the starting point for cloud contracts is usually the providers' standard terms and conditions, which are provider favorable and designed for high-volume, low-cost, standard, commoditized services on shared multi-client infrastructure. The five most heavily negotiated issues in a cloud contract are liability, performance metrics, security, termination rights, and termination assistance.

With respect to liability, cloud providers almost universally exclude or disclaim all liability for outages and data loss. Companies need to assess the type of information or data that will reside on the cloud and construct an appropriate liability provision. Cloud providers will accept liability, but it is typically capped, sometimes with different caps for different types of losses, and often limited by reference to amounts paid by the user in total or over a period such as a year, which is a common outsourcing liability construct. In addition, some cloud providers will agree to a higher percentage or longer period of fees for certain deals, especially, for example, if the fees were paid up front.

As with the limitations on liability issue, companies need to assess the type of information or data that will reside on the cloud and construct appropriate performance metrics or service levels. Assuring business continuity and disaster recovery (i.e., integrity and availability of cloud data and applications) are usually what is most important to businesses. Depending on the type of data or applications that reside in the cloud, companies also need to consider other service levels, including uptime/availability and restoration of data (including specifying both a recovery point objective and a recovery time objective). Note that many cloud providers reference service levels by linking to a website for details. Companies should clearly establish whether the service levels and other key terms can be amended by the cloud provider, and if, so whether the company will be provided notice and/or a right to terminate for substantive changes in the service levels.

Additionally, clients are almost universally concerned with security on the cloud. In most outsourcing deals, the provider is obligated to agree to specific security standards, to follow the client's security policies, and to permit audits or other broad inspection rights to assess compliance with various security requirements. Most cloud providers are unwilling to agree to these types of requirements. Given the use of shared infrastructure, cloud providers are not willing to provide full details of their security policies and practices to all prospective customers or even permit site visits. Moreover, cloud providers will not agree to comply with a user's security policy because where multiple users share standardized infrastructure, it is difficult if not impossible for providers to comply with each client's separate security policies, which might include different and even conflicting requirements. The best practice is to first determine what type of data will reside on the cloud. Depending on the data's sensitivity, clients may want more assurance on minimum-security levels than simply compliance with providers' own policies. For instance, some clients request that all data at rest and all connections be encrypted. In addition, if the provider is unwilling to disclose all of its security policies and protocols and/or otherwise provide for certain inspection or audit rights and the provider is unwilling to comply with a client's security policies, one alternative is an industry standard. The Cloud Security Alliance, Open Data Centre Alliance, and Cloud Industry forum have or are close to publishing cloud-specific security standards.

Finally, with respect to termination rights, the issue primarily arises in the context of a provider's right to terminate. In most outsourcing transactions, a provider's right to terminate will be very limited. A typical cloud agreement, however, will include immediate right to terminate or "suspend" services for material breach, breach of acceptable use policies (AUPs), or upon receiving third-party complaints regarding breach of their intellectual property rights. AUPs tend to be "take it or leave it" and are not often negotiated; most clients are primarily concerned with a provider's right to change the AUPs unilaterally. The best practice is to narrow these termination rights as much as possible. From a company's perspective, the trigger for each of these rights needs to be defined as objectively and precisely as possible. In addition, businesses should insist on standard termination rights—breach, change of control, breach of confidentiality, or intellectual property rights

In tandem with negotiating appropriate termination rights, companies should also focus on what happens on termination or expiration of the cloud services contract. Although most cloud providers do not offer any termination assistance services, businesses should focus on data availability and data portability. Specifically, businesses should specify in the cloud services contract how long (after termination or expiration) the data will be available on the cloud provider's systems. The standard protocol for most cloud providers is to delete all data immediately or after a short period (thirty days); longer periods must be specifically negotiated. Companies should also specifically negotiate how and in what format the data is returned. Data portability is often overlooked; businesses run the risk of dependence on one cloud provider's proprietary, service. If the service is terminated, ideally a business should be able to recover all its data in formats that are easily accessible, readable, and portable into other applications. Most cloud providers will commit to return a client's data in a standard format (typically CSV) on termination but to avoid unwanted surprises, the format of the data should be specified in the cloud services contract.

Multi-Provider Environments

A second trend in outsourcing is a growing use by businesses of multiple service providers in their environments. In the past, the prevailing delivery model was to contract with a single service provider that may have various subcontractors that assisted in delivering services, but from a business' perspective, was the single point of contact for any issues or failures. In recent years, in an effort to optimize the delivery of services, businesses have elected to diversify their portfolio of providers. In a recent survey, Gartner reports that in North America, client organizations on average engage 4.8 infrastructure service providers and 13.5 providers overall. Clearly, businesses are trending toward a best-of-breed approach with multiple providers in their environment. Although this trend has facilitated the introduction of new niche providers, it has also created (from a client perspective) a need for a coordination and integration of those services. To address these concerns, I think businesses need to consider four key issues: (i) integration sessions, (ii) enhanced terms and conditions related to operating in the multi-provider environment, (iii) operating level agreements, and (iv) shared service levels.

From applications and infrastructure to human resources and accounting, organizations have adopted the best-of-breed approach to sourcing. This optimization of service delivery at the functional level requires defined responsibilities and demarcation points to provide an integrated end-to-end delivery of services to the user. In my experience, prior to entering into a large-scale outsourcing agreement in a multi-provider environment, it is often necessary to facilitate discussions between all providers in the environment.

The underlying purpose of these facilitated "integration sessions" is to identify the various touch points between the providers in delivering the service to the client. The output of the various integration sessions will form the basis for the operating level agreements (which is discussed in more detail later). Integration sessions are primarily for the benefit of the service providers. Typically, the goals for a facilitated integration session are to (i) improve the service provider's solution by gaining an improved understanding of integration points (from the other service providers), (ii) reduce the number of unknowns and assumptions in a service provider's proposed solution, and (iii) accomplish a more complete assessment of risks in the environment (to minimize gaps, minimize overlaps, and reduce the premium associated with perceived risks in the environment). At the highest level, each service provider will be asked to provide details related to (i) service strategy and service design, (ii) transition activities, and (iii) service operation (steady-state processes).

The second recommendation relates to the terms and conditions that a service provider must commit to, to effectively operate in a multi-provider environment. First, the standard cooperation provision in a master service agreement must be expanded to address the existence of other service providers as well as contemplate the execution of operating level agreements between the various service providers. As a starting point, we typically use the following provision:

> *Service Provider acknowledges and agrees that it will deliver the Services to Customer in an environment in which there are various other Service Providers providing related Services to Customer ("Multi-Supplier Environment"). Service Provider acknowledges that its provision of the Services in a Multi-Supplier Environment requires significant integration, cooperation, and coordination of processes and procedures with other Service Providers. Attachment 6-C specifies certain Service Provider obligations to Customer related to the OLAs. In addition, Service Provider agrees to enter into OLAs with each other Service Provider that address joint operation, issue resolution, and joint governance of the delivery of the services. Each OLA will be substantially in the form of Exhibit [xx] and include terms that at a minimum address (i) document control and version information, (ii) authorizations, dates and signatures, (iii) objectives*

of the OLA, (iv) obligations of each party by Service Component, (v) governance, including an approach to managing the OLA that includes managing and coordinating issues, communications, and oversight responsibility, (vi) issue escalation and resolution procedures, (vii) procedures for oversight reporting and quality review, (viii) description of solution-based dependencies related to shared use of facilities, equipment, licenses, tools, systems, and other resources, and (ix) interdependency commitments. Within thirty (30) days of the later of (i) the Effective Date, or (ii) the Effective Date of the Master Services Agreement entered into between Customer and the Service Provider who is a counter-party to the OLA, Service Provider will submit a draft OLA to Customer for its review and comment. If, after 15 days from Customer's receipt of such draft, Customer has not provided comments to the OLA or otherwise requested an extension of the period for review, Service Provider may proceed with the proposed OLA. If Customer provides comments to the OLA, the Service Provider will address and resolve any questions or concerns Customer may have and resubmit the OLA to Customer. Customer will have an additional fifteen (15) days to review each resubmission following the same review process described above. Notwithstanding the terms of the applicable OLA or the approval of any OLA by Customer, Service Provider shall be and remain responsible and liable for any failure to perform in accordance with this Agreement or to comply with any duties or obligations imposed on Service Provider under this Agreement. Without limiting the foregoing, Service Provider warrants and covenants that in no event shall any provision of this Agreement, or any right or benefit of Customer or the Customer Customers provided for under this Agreement, be reduced, limited, or otherwise adversely affected (including through any increase in cost, Charge or expense, including taxes) as a consequence of the terms of an OLA.

The key component of this provision is that it expressly contemplates the use of operating level agreements (OLAs), including with respect to the governance of the overall service delivery to the business.

The third key consideration is the development and use of OLAs. OLAs create a contractual bond between service providers and are a component of the services each provider is obligated to deliver to the business. The OLAs clarify integration roles and responsibilities of each service provider and support enterprise service management processes and contracted service levels. There are three parts of a standard OLA. Part A consists of the obligations between service providers and client. Parts B and C provide the detail of the OLAs between the service providers.

OOLA Category	Purpose	Description
Part A *Contractual Framework*	• Obligations of service provider to client	• Codified in contract • Address procedural rules related to management and cooperation • Address changes and approval processes for OLA • Address inter/intra provider dispute management and escalation
Part B *Between Providers*	• Describes agreement between the parties • Recital language • Fundamental assumptions and interdependencies	• Acknowledgements of cooperation and reliance between providers (e.g., tool sharing) • Acknowledgement of mutual obligations to the client • Procedural rules established between service providers (including for the development of additional OLA elements in Part C)
Part C *Between Components*	• Specific OLA elements • Solution component specific	• Elements align with components of service management manual (SMM) and are solution-specific • Process descriptions/ parameters/ targets established between service providers • Role descriptions and operations management

		protocols established between service providers • MSI drives process development, including development and changes to OLA elements

The final consideration relates to service levels. With successful delivery of service to the business end user contingent upon multiple providers, attainment of certain service levels is a joint responsibility, and the service level methodology must recognize this dynamic. There are three categories of service levels, and only the fully shared category includes a single measurement that affects two service providers.

- Fully shared

  o Identical metric descriptions and targets for each provider
  o Single measurement affects two providers
  o Measurement approach and targets must remain identical through the term; however, crediting is distinct and based on individual provider's allocation, etc.

- Related

  o Address areas where MSI has enterprise responsibility
  o Measurements are based on similar pools of events but occur separately for each provider
  o Targets may fluctuate over the term

- Unique

  o Measure services specific to a provider

For fully shared service levels, both providers are affected in the event of a failure and will incur service level credits. However, the governance model should allow a service provider to demonstrate the extent of its response to the event (both proactive and reactive) in an effort to highlight to the business that appropriate measures and remedies have been implemented to offset the need for a credit.

Role of Governance in a Provider-Client Relationship

With an emerging interest in using multiple service providers, one issue that should also get renewed interest is effective governance of the various service providers in the environment. Although governance is often overlooked, it is vital to building a proper relationship between a business and a service provider. Unlike a typical M&A transaction, an outsourcing transaction establishes a dynamic, long-term relationship between a business and a service provider. The needs of the business purchasing the services will change over the term of the contract and as a result, the nature of the services being delivered and the technology used to deliver those services will also change. Add multiple service providers operating in the environment to the mix, and the complexity of governing the relationships increases exponentially. Although there are a number of different approaches to governance, the following five components should be addressed in every governance plan/model: (i) establishment of the various governance committees, (ii) roles and responsibilities of key governance team members, (iii) a decision/operating matrix, (iv) service management manual, and (v) escalation procedures. With respect to the team members, this will largely depend on the functions that are outsourced and the client's retained organization. The basic idea is to have analogs between the key business and service provider positions. Typically, the provider will have an account executive responsible for managing the overall relationship. The provider account executive will be supported by various positions supporting discrete functions (e.g., service delivery managers for each key area of service—service delivery manager-applications, service delivery manager infrastructure). In addition, there typically would also be a position for the transition manager (per functional area outsourced) and other key support roles (finance, contracts, and human resources). Additionally, a governance model will also establish various committees and the key responsibilities for such committees (e.g., executive committee, service delivery committee). An example of the typical components describing a committee are as follows:

Members

The service delivery committee will be composed.

Authority

All members of the service delivery committee:

- Review and approve, where possible, the short-term and long-term plans and activities with regard to the delivery of the services.
- Resolution of service delivery problems.
- Notification of all opportunities or issues that might result in the addition, deletion, or modification of the services, or the terms of the agreement, irrespective of which party initiates the notification.

Key Responsibilities

The responsibilities and authorities of the client and provider representatives will be determined and delegated in each case by the management committee and may include matters:

- Implement the transition plan and monitor the service delivery.
- The appropriate client service manager(s) and provider service delivery managers will carry out the day-to-day coordination of service delivery and will include other client representatives as required.
- Monitor critical deliverables and service levels.
- Coordinate and communicate day-to-day service delivery issues and address, co-coordinate, and prioritize the issues affecting the provision of the services to client.
- Review and escalate operational problems and issues in accordance with the policy and procedures manual.
- Review and schedule change requests in accordance with the change management process described in Attachment 2.1 (Cross-Functional Services) to Exhibit 2.
- Ensure efficient flow of documentation as required by the agreement.
- Submit issues concerning the relationship between the parties to the management committee for its guidance and recommendations.

- Submit reports as required and as defined in Exhibit 10 (Reports) to the management committee.

- Review and adjust the following, as directed by the management committee: (a) service levels; (b) continuous improvement and quality assurance measures; (c) customer satisfaction surveys; (d) audits; and (e) benchmarking results.

Reports

- Regional/management reports;
- Service levels and service delivery results (as required); and
- Minutes.

Meetings

The service delivery committee will meet (at a minimum) biweekly, and at other times as agreed between the parties, to review:

- Contract issues;
- Service delivery;
- Transition management (as required); and
- Transition/projects (as required).

In addition to establishing the committees and their roles and responsibilities described above, one particularly important component to good governance is a service management manual (SMM). The SMM will address a detailed description of the manner in which each of the services shall be performed by each provider, including: (i) documentation (including operations manuals, user guides, specifications, policies/procedures and disaster recovery/business continuity plans) to be created and/or maintained by provider in the course of performing the service; (ii) the specific activities to be undertaken by provider in connection with each service, including, where appropriate, the direction, supervision, monitoring, staffing, reporting, planning, and oversight activities to be performed by provider under this agreement; (iii) the checkpoint reviews, testing, acceptance, controls, and other procedures to be implemented and used to ensure service quality; (iv) the client-approved processes, methodologies, and controls to be implemented and used by provider to comply and confirm compliance with client rules and standards; (v) the processes, methodologies, and controls to be implemented and used by provider to comply and confirm compliance with applicable laws (including applicable privacy laws relating to the privacy and security of client data); and (vi) the processes, methodologies, and controls to be implemented and used by provider to implement client-approved billing structure changes. In addition, the SMM will include a description of the procedures for client, client customer, and provider interaction and communication, including call lists; procedures for and limits on direct communication by provider with client and client customer personnel; problem management and escalation procedures; change control procedures, acceptance testing and procedures, quality assurance procedures and checkpoint reviews; the project-formation process and implementation methodology; and the interfaces between and among client, client customers, and provider. The SMM should be a "critical deliverable" that is submitted by the service provider on a specified date (ideally prior to commencement of steady-state operations). In addition, the service provider should be obligated to maintain the currency of the SMM so that at any given point in time it provides an accurate description of the service provider's delivery processes and protocols and accurately describes the operating environment. As part of maintaining the currency of the SMM, if operating in a multi-service provider environment, the OLAs should also be maintained and updated at the same time any material changes or updates are made to the SMM.

Conclusion

Businesses will continue to turn to cloud computing delivery models. The price point and technology for cloud-enabled service delivery are compelling. As large service providers continue to invest, the cloud-related offering will become even more compelling. The competition among cloud service providers will continue to intensify and I expect that this result not only in better offerings (from an economic and technical perspective) but in an effort to distinguish themselves from the competition, it will also result in certain cloud service providers becoming more flexible in the terms and conditions that govern cloud-based offerings. I expect to see a shift to more flexible terms and conditions that will be more acceptable to large commercial and governmental entities. I also expect that a common or industry-standard security protocol to be established that will enable a broader expansion of cloud-based solutions to industries that are more sensitive to security concerns (e.g., banking, manufacturing, health care).

Businesses that are willing to use multiple-providers in their environment will also continue to grow. The best of breed approach has significant traction in the marketplace. This will result in a renewed emphasis on how to maximize value in the integrated environment (by using some of the best practices described above). I also believe there will be a renewed focus on governance. The traditional governance models will be enhanced and "integration" will become a vital cross-functional service. Interestingly, we have also started to see transactions where integration is provided as a stand-alone service under the auspices of a "multi-sourcing service integrator." Several Tier I outsourcing service providers have entire lines of business dedicated to these offerings. In fact, the state of Texas recently bid out a large infrastructure transaction and requested that bidders either provide infrastructure services in the traditional manner (e.g., mainframe, midrange, or data center) or alternatively bid to become the multi-source service integrator. This cutting-edge transaction has spawned a number of similar transactions.

Key Takeaways

- The best practice for managing cloud security concerns is to first determine what type of data will reside on the cloud.

- Regarding termination rights with cloud providers, the best practice is to narrow these rights as much as possible and to focus on the client's rights on termination (or expiration) of the agreement.

- Remember data portability in relation to termination rights. Ensure that if the service is terminated, all data can be recovered in formats that are easily accessible, readable, and portable into other applications, whether running internally or in another provider's cloud.

- The best practices for managing multi-sourcing include: integration sessions, enhanced terms and conditions related to operating in the multi-provider environment, operating level agreements, and shared service levels.

- Prior to entering into a large-scale outsourcing agreement in a multi-provider environment, it is often necessary to facilitate discussions between all providers in the environment.

Michael J. Brito, a partner with Akin Gump Strauss Hauer & Feld LLP, has significant experience in structuring, negotiating and drafting various types of agreements for complex technology transactions in the United States, Europe, Latin America, and Asia Pacific, including global information technology and business process outsourcing agreements, telecommunications outsourcing agreements, cloud computing and cloud services agreements, software development agreements, supply chain management agreements, licensing and marketing agreements, joint ventures, strategic alliances and teaming relationships. He has also been actively involved in various e-commerce transactions and enterprise-wide software licensing agreements (e.g., ERP systems).

What Companies Need to Know About Outsourcing Contracts

Peter Burns and Matt Karlyn

Partners

Cooley LLP

ASPATORE

Introduction

In this chapter, we will describe important principles and recent trends related to outsourcing in today's business environment and how to structure outsourcing programs and contracts.

Outsourcing has evolved in recent years and will continue to evolve based on factors including business cycles and climate, macro-economic conditions, technology, demographics, service provider industry composition, and politics, laws, and regulations. Understanding these factors can help companies procuring outsourcing services ensure that they minimize risks and are positioned for short- and long-term success.

Important Trends in Outsourcing

The time, effort, and costs exerted to select an outsourcing partner (commonly through an request for proposal (RFP) process), negotiate a contract with favorable terms, and transition services to the provider historically was measured in months and often years. It was not uncommon for this process to require twelve and even up to twenty-four months. Today, however, as deal sizes continue to shrink and companies diversify their vendor portfolio for outsourced services, the process is typically measured in weeks (or several months for more complex deals).

There are several factors driving this change. These include (i) past experiences with prior outsourcings have led to more streamlined outsourcing procurement and transition processes, (ii) shorter term (e.g., three years as opposed to ten years), (iii) smaller and more focused scope, and (iv) standardized business and technology practices in-house (e.g., fewer internally developed applications). Historically successful experiences with prior outsourcings have reduced certain "fears" about outsourcing at many companies. Shorter and smaller deals increase each party's incentive to do a deal quickly to reduce transaction costs relative to deal size. A shorter term and more flexibility with respect to termination and transition-out rights also reduce many of the risks associated with longer-term deals. And, standardized business applications and/or historically successful outsourcings have given many buyers the confidence to agree to work out certain operational and technical details during the transition phase and/or adopt the service provider's standard practices with fewer changes than they did historically. In short, outsourcing deals are becoming smaller and buyers are more educated, but outsourcing remains a complex area and buyers need to be mindful about the inherent risks associated with any outsourcing transaction and ensure that they do appropriate levels of due diligence and contingency planning as outsourcing, regardless of deal size or scope, still leads to major business interruptions and significant financial impact if not successfully executed.

Generally, in the last ten years, the duration of outsourcing deals has shrunk from seven to ten years to three to five years. Except in the more significant, multi-tower, full-scale information technology (IT) outsourcing transactions, it is uncommon today to have terms much longer than five years. This trend creates more transition and operational risks, because there are likely to be more transitions over time. But this trend also provides buyers more flexibility and options. Most buyers think the latter advantages offset the increased risks. However, even with shorter terms, there are still significant costs involved in transitioning to a new provider when a term expires. Therefore, buyers need to consider the fact that the buyer will likely desire to retain the incumbent service provider and therefore the incumbent service provider will have leverage to negotiate a renewal—which has a similar practical impact as a long-term initial deal.

Outsourcing deals have, over time, also become smaller in scope (e.g., a single functional service area as opposed to a multi-tower relationship). Historically, most IT outsourcing transactions included a wide range of information technology services (e.g., data center and server management, application maintenance and development, networks, end user computing and desk side services, and help desk). Similarly, most business process outsourcing deals were widespread across an organization (e.g., human resources, call center, finance and accounting). These services were provided by a single service provider. While this is still common in larger companies, and even smaller companies that are not comfortable managing a multi-vendor environment, many transactions in recent years are for a smaller discrete set of functions spread across several service providers. Buyers are therefore not getting a single service provider accountable for all services (e.g., a "single throat to choke") if something goes wrong and must internally manage a multi-sourced environment with several vendors. However, buyers are not exposed to as much risk if a single service provider has financial or performance problems. Accordingly, buyers need to ensure that these factors are carefully balanced when determining scope, and contracts must be structured to foster and require integration and coordination.

Buyers are also more willing to consider and accept a service provider's standard service delivery offering/solution and are not as inclined to insist on "lifting and shifting" their current operations and processes as-is to the service provider. As a result, it is easier and faster to negotiate the service delivery aspects of the contract and relationship. However, this process requires more thorough vendor selection and due diligence before the execution of the contract to ensure that that the provider's offering comports to the buyer's requirements and expectations (understanding that few changes to the environment will be made). This approach can also lead to more unexpected surprises and unplanned change order fees if buyers are not careful or the users are unwilling to adapt to the service provider's processes. Buyers need to proceed carefully and ensure their contracts including appropriate processes, protections, and options to address these situations on terms that are favorable to the buyer, including change control processes (and pricing for changes), pricing protections, and low cost options to switch to another service provider if necessary.

The number of outsourcing service providers capable of winning a deal has grown significantly in the last several years as well. Until recently, larger services providers won most outsourcing deals. Because there were only a handful of companies capable of servicing a multi-tower transaction over several years, if not decades, most deals involved companies such as IBM, Accenture, EDS/HP, ACS/Xerox, TCS, Infosys, or Wipro. Over the past several years, smaller providers offering services similar to the big providers, or niche services, have infiltrated the market and are offering services with favorable economic and contractual terms. This is all consistent with the trend of multi-sourcing (e.g., utilizing several services providers to provide a solution, rather than sole sourcing).

The emergence of cloud computing is also affecting the service offerings of traditional outsourcing firms and many new companies with cloud-based offerings are infiltrating the outsourcing market. Because many buyers are procuring more cloud-based services, including software as a service (SaaS) applications and utilizing fewer internally hosted applications, the scope and size of information technology outsourcings has been impacted. The software/application vendors themselves are hosting and supporting applications and may even offer business process outsourcing services related to their application.

All of this being said, buyers are still engaging in numerous and significant outsourcing transactions. Buyers who are currently outsourced are also frequently renegotiating deal terms and price to ensure that their deal remains current with the market, the buyer's requirements, and technological improvements. While the duration and scope of deals may be shorter and smaller, critical terms still need to be included in outsourcing contracts and scrutinized carefully. For example, buyers are paying particular attention to the privacy, security, and information management terms and practices of service providers regardless of deal duration or size. Buyers are also insisting on a greater degree of flexibility, including the ability to add and remove services, increase or decrease service volumes without penalties or minimums, engage third parties, insource, and terminate the transaction. Buyers also continue to focus on other critical terms such as supplier accountability for governance/relationship management, service levels, compliance, technological improvements over time, and transition services (both transition into a supplier and transition out of a supplier in the event of a termination event or expiration of the agreement). Service levels and detailed statements of work are critical to any outsourcing transaction, regardless of duration or scope.

Economic Factors Driving Recent Trends in Outsourcing

In the 1990s (and the early 2000s, to some extent), the US dollar was strong, and US labor costs were relatively high, which encouraged labor-based outsourcing. Today, there are still considerable economic advantages to sourcing offshore, but those advantages are not as significant as in the past. In addition, buyers are more aware of the additional administrative costs of having staff around the world (more governance, travel costs, etc.). Consequently, offshore outsourcing is now being done more selectively and onshoring (and even insourcing) is making a comeback.

The cheaper cost, availability, and reliability of cloud-based data center storage is commoditizing data storage (much like the telecom technology). Industries that process high volumes of personal and other sensitive data, however, are more reluctant to use "commoditized" cloud storage companies, as they desire more control, supervision, and input with respect to their sensitive data. This trend seems to be accelerating with growing concerns over data security.

Ten or more years ago, many outsourcing deals were pseudo-financing deals where companies were reducing expenses on their profit and loss (P&L) statements, reducing assets on their balance sheets, and/or receiving "deferred fees" (pseudo-loans) from service providers through "financial engineering." Because (i) the costs of IT assets (mainframes, servers, etc.) have been reduced with respect to the amount of data processed, (ii) there are more rigorous accounting standards required in a Sarbanes-Oxley (SOX) world for both buyers and service providers, and (iii) buyers are happy with shorter-term deals, fewer outsourcing deals include these components. Outsourcing vendors are also less willing to act as financing companies for their clients in today's capital markets as it just does not make sense for them to do so anymore.

Key Outsourcing Objectives

Outsourcing objectives vary considerably by deal, but the usual objectives include the following:

- A general reorganization of the outsourced functions that have become stagnant or out of alignment with the company's business
- Labor arbitrage
- Improved processes
- Ability to leverage best practices, new technology, current knowledge, regulatory compliance solutions, and other turn-key solutions from the vendor
- The ability to more rapidly scale and adopt
- Access to a skilled technology staff
- Preference to manage a vendor as opposed to managing a staff and related payroll/benefits

- Cost reduction/containment
- Quality improvement

Companies are generally looking to outsource what they know a service provider can do well (or they cannot do internally following an M&A event). This strategy may be based on experiences, including those of internal staff members who have undergone prior outsourcings, or arise from insights the buyer acquires from advisor and consultants who have worked with other companies.

Today, very few companies are looking to outsource to a vendor that does not already have deep skills and resources in a particular function/process. Historically, that was less the case, as many companies were willing to outsource to transfer staff and assets, and the service provider wanted to acquire resources to service many clients with mixed success.

Best Practices for Choosing Appropriate Outsourcing Providers

Key considerations when choosing appropriate outsourcing providers include the following:

- Service delivery and technical capabilities
- Integration and interoperability with the buyer's organization and its other outsourcing service providers
- References from other clients
- The cultural fit between the organizations, strong executive relationships, and strong relationships between day-to-day senior management
- Domain knowledge about the buyer's industry
- Whether the service provider has a complementary geographical footprint to the buyer

It is also essential that buyers consider whether being one of many customers for the service provider is acceptable, or if they want to be an anchor customer for the service provider. That preference must be taken into consideration when selecting the right service provider and management personnel. It is also a good idea to "compare apples to apples" through the RFP, involve competent outsourcing and technology lawyers and consultants early on in the process including during the RFP stage of the transaction, and carefully manage the selection process to find the best fit and not lose leverage.

Before entering into an outsourcing relationship, a company should consider the following:

- The financial health of the service provider and the likelihood of the service provider being acquired or merging with another service provider and the impact of that type of event
- What responsibility/power/influence the account team has in the service provider's organization
- The cultural, communication, and work style fit between the buyer company's staff and the service provider's staff
- How other clients have gotten along with the service provider in terms of meeting expectations, early terminations, contract renewals, and disputes (informal or formal)

Structuring an Outsourcing Contract

Outsourcing contracts are typically structured as master services agreements with a variety of schedules and exhibits. Appendix B sets forth a checklist and summary of key contractual terms to consider for outsourcing contracts. Appendix C describes typical schedules and exhibits that are referenced by and incorporated into the outsourcing contract. The schedules and exhibits are designed to be flexible to address operational additions, deletions, or changes that may occur over time.

Terms and Conditions

The terms and conditions to a master outsourcing services agreement includes all of the legal terms and conditions applicable to both the buyer and supplier. This commonly includes critical provisions such as the supplier warranties, indemnities, limitations of liability, service definition, termination rights, dispute resolution procedures, and choice of law. The purpose of this document includes the following:

- Set forth the general legal framework of the relationship
- Identify high level objectives and expectations of the buyer
- Allocate risk
- Provide for fair and reasonable remedies if a party does not perform
- Ensures legal and regulatory compliance
- Protects against changes and unforeseeable circumstances
- Address termination and exit events, rights, and planning, including reverse transition
- Defines procedures in the event the parties get into a dispute

The negotiation of the terms and conditions is typically led by attorneys with active involvement of both the buyer's and service provider's senior management.

Schedules and Exhibits

The schedules and exhibits to the master outsourcing services agreement detail specifics relating to the outsourcing relationship. Lawyers from both the buyer and supplier as well as subject matter experts from both sides are actively engaged in drafting and negotiating these documents.

Schedules and exhibits are an essential part of any master outsourcing services agreement regardless of the size, scope, or duration of the outsourcing transaction. These documents describe the specific services and technology, service levels, pricing, and other particulars of each transaction.

From a technology perspective, one or more schedules or exhibits will:

- Describe what is required to be done by each party on a day-to-day basis
- Identify the required experiences and skill set of the service provider's personnel
- Identify particular technology and integration points

From a commercial perspective, one or more schedules will include the following:

- A pricing model, which will drive the service provider's behavior and therefore should be carefully analyzed
- Caps and/or sharing mechanisms to align risks relating to inflation, deflation, foreign currency, or other factors
- If necessary, productivity and resource/personnel mix (e.g., ratios of onshore to offshore personnel; ratios of senior to junior personnel) commitments to ensure that overall fees are reasonable
- Mechanisms to increase, decrease, remove, change, and benchmark services and fees based on the evolving nature of the buyer, M&A activity, and the market

Best Practices for Ensuring the Provider Adheres to the Outsourcing Agreement

It is important to ensure that the service provider is adhering to the outsourcing agreement. This is typically done through periodic governance meetings and reports as well as audits. Key areas to consider are:

Price: The pricing schedule in most outsourcing transactions is a detailed document that specifies the price, often on a unit basis, for services provided. This schedule will often include details with respect to what the buyer is required to pay to the extent they exceed or underutilize the expected number of units. These charges should be reconciled against invoices and the services actually being provided. Buyers should also make sure they are not "receiving" unnecessary services and require (and incent) service providers to eliminate unnecessary services and manage demand through change control and cost reduction programs and procedures. Pricing reviews and benchmarking should happen periodically, as described in the master outsourcing services agreement, to ensure the supplier's pricing remains consistent with market-based pricing for similar deals, especially in longer-term transactions.

Service quality and continuous improvement: Outsourcing agreements typically include a robust service level schedule with a performance credit structure compensating a buyer in the event that the service provider is not able to perform the services at some minimum or expected level. Buyers need to require service providers to provide reports on their service level performance and verify that those reports are accurate. Buyers should also insist on rights to add and change service levels, re-weight credits for mal-performance based on changing business priorities, and adjust the service levels for technology changes and continuous improvement expectations.

Continued alignment with the client's business objectives: Outsourcing agreements typically include a very clear statement and detailed list articulating the buyer's business objectives. These objectives are also typically referenced and reported against pursuant to contractual schedules pertaining to governance and contract management meetings and reporting. To the extent the parties are not aligned, that must be corrected through governance, change control, and amendments. This is an ongoing process requiring monthly, quarterly, and annual meetings at varying levels of both parties' organizations.

Security: Agreements involving sensitive data will contain extensive requirements with respect to privacy, security, and information management and those requirements must be constantly monitored by the buyer (and third-party security auditors and experts) throughout the course of the relationship. Regardless of the size or duration of the transaction, this is not an area to be overlooked and a supplier's practices with respect to security should be scrutinized carefully. Outsourcing contracts should contain requirements with respect to: the protection of the buyer's data; warranties and indemnities with respect to data privacy and security; data breach notification processes; where (e.g., onshore or offshore) and how (encrypted) data can be stored, processed, or transmitted; insurance; privacy audits and ethical hacks; compliance certifications and safe harbors; and special remedies and limitation of liability exclusions for data breaches, as applicable.

Compliance with applicable regulations: Outsourcing agreements frequently contain warranties with respect to the service provider's conformance to applicable laws and regulations, which must be regularly monitored by buyers in regulated industries.

Contingency planning: Outsourcing agreements should also contain detailed requirements with respect to maintaining documentation and capabilities to facilitate a transition of the services back to the client or a third party in the event of a termination, force majeure event, or other disruption in the services. This requires pre-planning, information sharing, and testing on a periodic basis.

Best Practices for Maintaining Leverage Over Time

To ensure that leverage with respect to an outsourcing agreement is maintained over the years in the buyer's favor, it is a good idea to seek shorter-term deals with low termination fees so that the threat of non-renewal or early termination is real. Adding transition services provisions is also critical to protect the buyer in the event of an eventual transition. However, buyers should also understand that shorter-term deals can be more expensive and transitioning can be difficult and costly even if a buyer has the right to do so and has maintaining appropriate contingency plans. Longer-term deals will often look attractive due to price, but careful scrutiny with respect to termination and other provisions ensuring buyer flexibility is required.

Leverage can also be maintained by establishing a multi-sourced environment where service providers have an opportunity to expand the scope of their relationship with the buyer if the service provider is doing well (or shrink the scope by giving discretionary project work to another service provider if the service provider performs poorly). For example, the buyer should provide service providers opportunities to bid on new scope/projects if they perform well. Similarly, if the service provider performs poorly, a tacit threat of decreased scope, non-renewal, and/or termination can motivate a service provider to perform better. In other words, buyers should utilize incentives and penalties (or "sticks and carrots") wherever possible to manage the relationship. If the buyer has other sources capable of providing the outsourced services without huge transition risks or expenses, service providers will have incentive to perform well.

Regular communication with your service provider is also critical throughout the term of the relationship. This should be undertaken and led by senior executives of each party and permeate through all levels of each organization. These processes should be well defined in the contract (usually in a well-developed and precisely drafted governance exhibit) and not overlooked (even when everything is going well and even in smaller transactions).

Conclusion: Upcoming Trends in Outsourcing

So, what will the future hold? It is hard to say, but certainly look for the following trends:

- A continued trend toward multi-sourced environments
- The rise of "prime" or "lead integration" outsourcers to manage SaaS and cloud providers and/or integrate and oversee other niche outsourcers as multi-sourcing expands
- Growth of more US-led outsourcing to (i) complement offshore outsourcing, (ii) reduce risk, and (iii) implement more advanced technology and better manage data and regulatory issues (e.g., the Health Insurance Portability and Accountability Act (HIPAA), Gramm-Leach-Bliley Act (GLBA), etc.).

These trends will be largely driven by the growth of cloud-based offerings, the desire of buyers to choose "best of breed" service providers and solutions, global economics, data security concerns, and the desire of buyers to maintain flexibility.

Key Takeaways

- Outsourcing deals are becoming shorter in duration and smaller in scope, but still need to be scrutinized and carefully negotiated.
- Buyers are increasingly deferring the definition of certain operational details until transition to more quickly execute deals. But this requires: careful vendor selection and due diligence; rigorous ongoing governance and oversight; and detailed contractual procedures and protections to mitigate the risks inherent in such a strategy.
- Buyers are regularly utilizing multi-sourced outsourcing environments, which requires integration, coordination, and collaboration and provides for greater flexibility.
- Privacy and data security concerns need to be carefully analyzed and addressed.
- Buyers must preserve flexibility and leverage to address changes in the marketplace through renegotiations and the renewal process.

Peter Burns is a partner in the Technology Transactions and Clean Energy and Technologies practice groups and a member of the Cooley LLP Business department. He initially joined the Technology Transactions Group in 2000 and, after several years as an antitrust litigator, rejoined the Firm in early 2005. He is resident in the Palo Alto office, where he focuses on outsourcing and transactions involving the acquisition, development and commercialization of technology.

Matt Karlyn is a partner in the Technology Transactions practice group and a member of the Cooley LLP Business department. He joined the Firm in 2013 and is resident in the Boston office. Mr. Karlyn regularly advises companies on all matters involving the procurement and use of information technology in business and outsourcing initiatives, including drafting RFPs and managing the RFP process; vendor selection; developing, drafting and negotiating contracts; setting service levels and other performance criteria; advising on pricing strategies and alternatives; drafting and negotiating project management and governance terms and conditions; and assisting in the overall management of the transaction and transition process.

Acknowledgment: The authors would like to acknowledge the assistance of Mark Petry, special counsel with Cooley LLP.

APPENDICES

APPENDIX A

SAMPLE MARKET CURRENCY PROCEDURES

This is Exhibit X, Market Currency Procedures, to that certain Master Services Agreement, dated as of [_____], between [Customer] and [Provider].

1. Definitions. Unless otherwise defined herein, each term defined in the Master Agreement and its Exhibits, including the "Definitions" Exhibit to the Master Agreement, shall have the same meaning in this Exhibit.

2. Benchmarking Process and Procedures.

2.1 Initiating Benchmarking. The Benchmarking Process may be initiated by Customer at any time after the [first] anniversary of the Effective Date by giving at least thirty days' prior notice to Service Provider. At the option of Customer, Customer may initiate the Benchmarking Process for all, or a portion of, the Services (the "Benchmarked Services"). Customer shall select and retain the Benchmarker from the list of Benchmarkers set forth in the Transaction Document.

2.2 Benchmarking Process Methodology. Customer, Service Provider and the Benchmarker shall conduct the benchmarking process according to the following methodology:

(a) The Benchmarker shall select a sampling of other outsourced organizations that the Benchmarker determines in its professional judgment share substantially similar attributes with respect to size, investments, geography, scope and nature of overall services, skill sets, quality standards and Service Levels, technology, and payment and performance credit structure (the "Comparators"). There shall be six Comparators or such lesser number (but no less than three) if the Comparator information available to the Benchmarker is comprised of a lesser number of Comparators. The Benchmarker shall make adjustments to the Comparators as it determines in its professional judgment to be necessary to permit a normalized comparison.

(b) For each Comparator used to calculate the Benchmark Results, the Benchmarker shall disclose to Customer and Service Provider the demographic data (e.g., the total number of Service resource units and/or other basis on which Charges are based, a general description of the quality of services and service environment and other similar data) reasonably required for the Parties to understand the basis upon which the Benchmarker selected the Comparators. Due to the confidential nature of Comparator data and nondisclosure agreements to which such data may be subject, the Benchmarker shall not be required to disclose the name of the Comparators, or other potentially identifying information that the Benchmarker believes may compromise the confidentiality of the data.

(c) The Benchmarker shall compare each Comparator's contracted charges, service levels and scope with Service Provider's contracted Charges, Service Levels and scope with respect to the subject Services. The Benchmarker shall compare the applicable Service Levels with the Comparator's committed service levels for each element of the Benchmarked Services where the Benchmarker determines that such comparison is meaningful and objective.

(d) The Benchmarker shall use normalization techniques that the Benchmarker deems appropriate in its professional judgment to use to make such adjustments. The Benchmarker shall fully explain its normalization techniques to Service Provider and Customer.

(e) Customer and Service Provider agree (A) that the Benchmarker will conduct the Benchmarking Process in accordance with the Benchmarker's own policies, methodologies and practices applied in the exercise of its professional judgment, (B) to consult with each other regularly and cooperate reasonably with the Benchmarker in the Benchmarking Process activities, and (C) that Customer shall serve as the Benchmarker's primary point of contact; provided, however, that Customer shall provide Service Provider with the opportunity to participate in any substantive discussions with the Benchmarker that relate to Service Provider's role in the Benchmarking Process.

(f) Customer will be permitted to disclose price and Customer's cost information under this Agreement to the Benchmarker. Service Provider shall not be obligated to disclose to the Benchmarker data with respect to any other customers of Service Provider, internal costs and margin (including effort details for fixed-priced Services) and employee-information.

(g) All material information provided to and obtained from the Benchmarker shall be provided to both Service Provider and Customer unless otherwise agreed by the Parties. Such information shall be deemed to be Confidential Information of the providing Party (or, if such information originated with the Benchmarker and is not the Confidential Information of either Party, of both Parties) under the Agreement and shall be subject to the confidentiality agreement executed with the Benchmarker.

2.3 Benchmark Results.

(a) The Benchmarker shall provide the data, analysis and findings, including any supporting documentation, for the subject Services to Service Provider and Customer as appropriate throughout the Benchmarking Process.

(b) The Benchmarker shall prepare the complete "Benchmark Results" (i.e., a normalized analysis of the Comparators charges to the Charges) promptly, but no later than ninety days after the commencement of the Benchmarking Process by the Benchmarker. If the Benchmarker is for any reason unable to complete the Benchmarking Process within the time period set forth in this Section, the Parties will reasonably extend such period to allow the Benchmarker to complete the Benchmarking Process.

2.4 Benchmark Review; Limited Adjustments to Charges. Upon completion of the Benchmarking Process, Customer and Service Provider shall review the Benchmark Results during the 30 day period following delivery to Customer and Service Provider of the Benchmark Results, and shall in good faith discuss any suggested adjustments to the Service Levels or Charges under the Agreement. Notwithstanding the results of the foregoing discussions, if the Benchmark Results show that the relevant Charges are less than 5 percent higher than the normalized charges paid by the average of the Comparators that were the subject of such Benchmarking Process, then there will be no change in the Charges. If the results show that the relevant Charges are between 5 percent and 20 percent greater than the normalized charges paid by the average of the Comparators in the first quartile of the Comparators, then the relevant Charges for the subject Services will be automatically reduced such that Service Provider's Charges are 5 percent higher than the normalized charges paid by the average of the Comparators. If the results show that the relevant Charges are more than 20 percent higher than the normalized charges paid by the average of the Comparators in the first quartile of the Comparators, then Service Provider will (i) offer an alternative proposal for Customer's consideration for further adjustments to either the scope of the subject Services, Service Levels or Charges and (ii) offer to decrease the relevant Charges by 15 percent. If Customer rejects Service Provider's proposal, Customer will have the right to terminate the Agreement for convenience without payment of any Termination Charge or other charges however described, and Service Provider shall decrease the relevant Charges by 15 percent for the remainder of the period that Service Provider provides any of the subject Services. Any adjustment to the Charges shall be made effective as of the first date on which such benchmark is requested by Customer in writing.

2.5 Access and Confidentiality. Any Benchmarker engaged by Customer shall agree in writing with Customer to be bound by the applicable confidentiality and security provisions specified in the Agreement. Each Party shall co-operate fully with the Benchmarker and shall provide reasonable access to the Benchmarker during such effort to permit Benchmarker to perform the Benchmarking.

2.6 Cooperation and Assistance. Each Party will provide, and ensure that its subcontractors (excluding in the case of Customer, Service Provider and its subcontractors) provide, all necessary cooperation, information, documents and assistance reasonably required to perform the Benchmarking.

2.7 No Increase in Charges/Decrease in Service Levels. The Benchmarking Process shall not result in any increase in any Charges to Customer or decrease in the number, type or degree of Service Levels.

Courtesy of Randall S. Parks, Hunton & Williams LLP

APPENDIX B

CHECKLIST AND SUMMARY OF KEY CONTRACTUAL TERMS TO CONSIDER FOR OUTSOURCING CONTRACTS

Topic	Typical Position
Who may receive services	
Potential Service Recipients	Customer Any Customer affiliate (e.g., 50% ownership rights) Customer's joint venture partners, customers and vendors to the extent applicable
Local Country Agreements	Customer may require Service Provider to cause its global affiliates to enter into direct local country/regional agreements with Customer affiliates (e.g., EU, APAC, NA etc.) These agreements should only address unique requirements of those regions (e.g., tax, personnel/human resources, local laws)
Services	
Generally	Transition Transformation (e.g., new technology or reengineering) Services described in statements of work (SOWS), including [_____] Implied and historical services by employees/contractors even if not described Services service provider provides for other similarly situated customers Exit/termination assistance
Exclusivity / Minimums	Non-exclusive - Customer may retain third parties to do similar work. Service Provider will cooperate with these entities. No explicit minimums
Acquisitions and Divestitures	Acquired entities can be brought into scope through normal pricing mechanisms as a service recipient Divested entities can continue to receive services for up to 12-24 months under this agreement

Topic	Typical Position
Personnel	
Re-badged Customer Personnel	None, unless required by law or # and geographies Transfer terms per Schedule [S] (retention period, compensation, etc) Cost of severance/redundancy borne by [____]
Service Provider Key Personnel	Retention and dedication to Customer Right to interview and approve replacements 12-24 month restriction on transferring personnel to Customer competitors Customer has right to require Service Provider to remove personnel (mal-performance, unprofessionalism, suspected security breach)
Service Levels	
Potential Penalties	5-15% at risk each month 100-250% weighting
Evolution of SLAs	Unilateral right for Customer to change weighting allocations among service levels Right to add new service levels based on baselining and industry data Continuous improvement based on past performance
Commercials	
Fees	Model to be described in Schedule C Default currency (USD) COLA/ECA: [Index XXX], 50% share of increase, not to exceed [2-5]% in any year
Payment Terms	NET 30-60 days Arrears for both fixed and variable monthly fees (but many vendors seek net 30 with base fees invoiced at the beginning of the month)
Disputed Fees	Customer has the right to short pay with respect to disputed amounts
Benchmarking	Parties to periodically revisit prices relative to the market Customer has the right to engage a third party to benchmark the fees with respect to the market If Service Provider fees in excess of best quartile, Customer may receive a price reduction or exit at a reduced termination fee No increases

Topic	Typical Position
Term	
Term	3-5 year initial term Option to extend for up to 24 months thereafter at Customer's option
Termination for cause	Broad termination for cause rights to benefit Customer (uncured material breach, uncured transition delays, repeated SLA failures etc.) Service Provider termination rights limited to non-payment of undisputed fees

Termination for pure-Convenience	Only Customer can terminate for convenience
	Customer may terminate in whole or by part
	Customer must give 60 days notice
	Termination for convenience charges apply and consist of
	    Unamortized investments and deferred charges (*if any*) itemized in a schedule to the contract
	    Wind-down expenses (e.g., severance, 3rd party contracts and leases)
	    No lost profits
	    which generally decline over the term and are subject to a cap for planning purposes.

Other Customer Termination Rights	Customer may also terminate for the following events with reduced or no termination for convenience fees: Prolonged force majeure disasters Regulatory issues Service Provider financial condition Service Provider insolvency Change in law materially impacting economics of the transaction Customer's change in control
Termination for Service Provider Change of Control	Customer has the option to terminate due to Service Provider' change of control. If Customer terminates for this reason, no termination fees apply
Termination Assistance	Following any termination, Service Provider to provide continuation and transition assistance services for up to 12-24 months

Topic	Typical Position
	Robust termination assistance documentation and rights (e.g., procedure manuals, source code, hire personnel, option to buy-back assets)
Liability and other Legal Provisions	
General Limitations of Liability	Indirect and consequential damages (e.g., business loss) are generally not recoverable Liabilities generally cannot exceed 12-24 months fees
Exceptions	Fraud and willful misconduct Gross negligence and recklessness Third party indemnity claims Service Provider' termination or refusal to perform services Confidentiality and data breaches Service Provider' breaches with respect to insurance and legal non-compliance Service level credits and milestone credits
Choice of Law	Customer state or a neutral state

Courtesy of Peter Burns and Matt Karlyn, Cooley LLP

APPENDIX C

OVERVIEW OF TYPICAL EXHIBITS AND SCHEDULES

Document	Title	Primary Purpose
Exhibit 1	Defined Terms	Centralizes certain commonly used terms.
Exhibit 2	Form Confidentiality Agreement	Confidentiality template to be used with certain third party contractors who will receive confidential information.
[Exhibit 3	Service Provider Parent Guarantee] *[If applicable]*	Requires Service Provider's owner/parent to be liable for Service Provider's performance and liabilities.
[Exhibit 4	Local Country Agreement]*[If applicable]*	Unique agreement directly between the local affiliates in a country for employment/asset transfers, tax, or other reasons. These local country agreements are typically administrative, only a few pages in length, and incorporate the other provisions of the agreement.
Schedule A	Statements of Work	Describes the services and solution to be provided by the Service Provider.
Schedule A-1	[Tower 1 SOW]	Certain services are logically grouped to facilitate management, pricing, and terminations
Schedule A-2	[Tower 2 SOW]	
Schedule A-[n]	Critical Services	Identifies certain critical services previously described. If these critical services are not performed, Customer has specialized termination rights.
Schedule A-[n]	In-Flight Projects *[If applicable]*	Identifies in-process projects existing prior to the outsourcing that the Service Provider will complete.

Document	Title	Primary Purpose
Schedule B	Service Level Methodology	Generally describes processes for measuring and reporting performance, changes to performance standards, and the consequences of Service Provider's failure to meet theses standards.
Schedule B-1	Service Level Matrix	Table setting out specific service level performance standards, metrics, classifications, weightings, etc.
Schedule B-2	Service Level Measuring Tools	Describes how specific service levels are measured and the tools associated with those measurements.
Schedule C	Fee Methodology	Generally describes the pricing model(s), annual changes to the prices, and termination fees.
Schedule C-1	Base Fees by Tower	Table setting out fixed fees for certain services
Schedule C-2	Resource Units and Volume Baselines	Table setting out variable pricing metrics and estimated volumes
Schedule C-3	ARC and RRC Rates	Table setting out variable rates if actual volumes are greater than or less than the estimated volume (i.e., baseline)
Schedule C-4	Financial Responsibility Matrix	Table describing financial, operational, and administrative responsibilities for facilities, equipment, software, third parties, and people.
Schedule C-5	Transition [and Transformation] Service Fees	Fees for transition and transformation, if applicable. Typically, these fees are invoiced on a milestone acceptance basis.
Schedule C-6	Invoice Specification	Invoice form or template.

Document	Title	Primary Purpose
Schedule C-7	Rate Card	Table setting out certain default fees (per hour or FTE) for certain services (e.g., special projects). Typically used as a negotiation starting point.
Schedule C-8	Termination Fees	Table setting out costs/fees (or caps) that may apply if the Customer terminates before the end of the term by year/month.
Schedule C-9	Inflation Sensitivity Factors *[If applicable]*	Identifies the extent to which specific services are subject to inflation / deflation adjustments, if any. Labor intensive services are typically more sensitive to inflation index changes than capital intensive services.
[Schedule C-10	Financial Base Case] *[If applicable]*	Sets out the Customer's resources and estimated cost components for the services that are similar to those required by the Service Provider. Typically, Service Provider is required to provide resources/services that are referenced in the base case.
[Schedule C-11	Personnel Projection Matrix] *[If applicable]*	Estimates Service Provider's required staffing level and mix, including on/off shore mix, experience level, and re-badged percentages by year. Typically, this isn't a binding estimate, but Service Provider is not generally permitted to materially deviate from this estimate unless otherwise agreed.
Schedule D	Governance	Identifies key contract management protocols including, roles, meetings, committees, etc.
Schedule E	Change Control Procedures	Describes the process for changing the services and agreement.

Document	Title	Primary Purpose
Schedule F	Transition [and Transformation] Methodology	Describes how Service Provider will assume responsibility for and transform, if applicable, the Services and related resources. Subsidiary schedules will identify due dates, plans, Customer dependencies (e.g., knowledge transfer, on-site workspace for Service Provider), and remedies (e.g., credits payable to Customer) for not meeting such due dates.
Schedule G	Disaster Recovery and Business Continuity Plans	Describes disaster recovery and business continuity requirements, including recovery time and point objectives.
Schedule H	Audits	Describes Customer's audit rights, audit restrictions, and Service Provider's audit related requirements (e.g., annual SAS 70 Type II).
Schedule I	Insurance	Describes Service Provider's insurance policies and limits.
Schedule J	Defined Reports	Identifies certain reports and reporting frequencies.
Schedule K	Key Personnel	Identifies high level and key Service Provider positions and personnel that are subject to specialized provisions in the Agreement, including re-assignment.
Schedule L	Service Locations	Identifies places of performance and receipt, as applicable, of Services.
Schedule M	Market Currency (Benchmarking) Methodology	Generally describes processes and procedures designed to encourage the Service Provider to stay current with evolving technology, market prices, etc.
Schedule N	Customer Policies and Procedures	Identifies and groups Customer's existing policies and procedures that Service Provider will comply with.

Document	Title	Primary Purpose
Schedule O	Approved Subcontractors	Identifies pre-approved subcontractors that Service Provider may utilize on the account.
Schedule P	Technical Architecture	Identifies key technical and process related requirements and resources
Schedule Q	Competitors	Identifies Customer's (and typically Service Provider's) competitors. These lists may change over the term. Typically, Service Provider's cannot redeploy certain key personnel to Customer's competitors and Customer cannot use Service Provider competitors as auditors or benchmarkers.
Schedule R	Third Party Contracts	Identifies contracts that are either managed by or assigned to the Service Provider.
Schedule S	Human Resources Transfer Provisions *[If Applicable]*	Describes how the parties are transferring and/or allocating risks and costs related to the transfer(or termination) of employees as a result of the outsourcing. This schedule is particularly relevant if European employees are impacted.

Courtesy of Peter Burns and Matt Karlyn, Cooley LLP

ASPATORE